ZERO
A6M

H. P. Willmott

CHARTWELL BOOKS INC

A Bison Book

First published in the USA by
Chartwell Books Inc.
A Division of Book Sales Inc.
110 Enterprise Avenue
Secaucus, New Jersey 07094

Produced by
Bison Books Limited
4 Cromwell Place
London SW7

ISBN: 0-89009-322-9
Library of Congress Catalog Card Number 79-57099

Printed in Hong Kong

Page 1: Zero A6M2s on board a Japanese carrier await the signal to
take off for the Pearl Harbor attack.
Pages 2-3: A restored Zero A6M5a Model 52.
Pages 4-5: A captured Zero A6M2.

CONTENTS

CONCEPTS AND PROBI

In wars on either side of the turn of the nineteenth century Japan successfully defeated nations that on paper were infinitely more powerful than herself. In both wars, against the decaying empires of China (1894–95) and Russia (1904–1905), Japan faced enemies whose economic resources, manpower reserves and territorial area were greatly superior to her own; yet in both wars she triumphed. In both wars she followed the same basic blueprint for success. She recognized from the beginning her inability to defeat the Manchu and Romanov dynasties completely: Japan's aims in both wars were somewhat more limited. She sought to secure a position of strength against which her enemies, committed to the attack and feeding in their reserves in a piecemeal manner, would expend their effort in vain until such a time that both, tiring of the struggle and realizing the political, economic and strategic futility of persisting in wars that could not be carried to the Japanese homeland, came to accept compromise peaces. These peaces confirmed most of Japan's prewar objectives.

In both wars most of the fighting took place on land but the basis of Japan's victories was sea power. In both conflicts, attacking without the formality of a declaration of war, Japan quickly secured command of the seas. Thus in each of her wars Japan was able to impose a close blockade of the enemy. The aim of this was to prevent the movement of the enemy's fleet or, in the event of movement that could not be prevented, to force battle. The means Japan employed to secure command of the seas and to impose an effective blockade involved the use of both surprise and locally superior forces. It was the close blockade that enabled the Japanese to land and then to sustain armed forces on the continental mainland without any real danger of enemy interference. Nevertheless, to a Japan

poor in resources, underindustrialized and short of trained reservists, the securing and maintenance of command of the seas was not a task that fell primarily on the battlefleet. In accordance with Sino–Japanese notions of the preservation, intact, of one's main strength as far as that was possible, the main part of the battlefleet was held back, ready to give battle, but only committed to battle at the time of major crisis – 'the decisive battle,' beloved of strategists, particularly before 1914.

The cautious employment of the battlefleet was even more marked in the course of the Russo–Japanese war than it had been ten years earlier in the Sino–Japanese conflict. This was the result of two considerations. The first was the loss of capital ships on mines outside the main Russian base of Port Arthur; this made the Japanese doubly wary of risking major units. The second consideration was the fact that the Russians had much greater strength in depth than the Chinese, and the Japanese had to hold back forces to meet the Russian challenge that materialized in the form of the Baltic Fleet. In these circumstances the task of securing and then exercising command of the seas fell to Japan's light, small, expendable and easily replaced ships. The real function of these ships, in addition to their routine role of imposition and maintenance of the blockade, the sustaining of the army ashore and the giving of fire support to military operations where needed, was to ensure that any enemy force encountered would be engaged and defeated. This was the best that could be hoped for; the Japanese accepted that the defeat of enemy units might prove beyond the capacity of her light craft. But if the defeat of the enemy could not be brought about, then it was essential that he be subjected to disproportionately heavy losses that would cause either a faltering of his resolve or

EMS

allow the hitherto-restrained battlefleet to bring about the enemy's complete destruction under conditions of maximum advantage and safety to itself. The whole of Japanese naval strategy in these wars was, after the initial assault phase, defensive in its character. The backbone of the fleet and the capital ships were held back, and the brunt of the fighting (on the peripheries where the enemy's counteractions were met) fell on small gunboats and cruisers – cheap craft, capable of quick and inexpensive replacement.

'Cheap craft, capable of quick and inexpensive replacement' – the phrase is not without ambiguity and irony in its application to the Mitsubishi A6M Zero-sen. But it cannot be denied that in the Japanese concept of war this aircraft – and indeed all aircraft – fell into this 'expendable' category. As the 1920s slipped into the 1930s and the power of naval aviation grew, the Japanese were not slow to appreciate that aircraft in general and carrier-borne aircraft in particular provided ideal instruments, both offensively and defensively, for carrying

Above: **Zero fighters were the striking arm of the Japanese Imperial Navy at the beginning of the war.**
Below: **A Zero A6M2 in flight.**

Above: The *Shokaku* was laid down as a direct counterpart to the second-generation American carriers.

out the 1894–1905 blueprint. In the event of war the Imperial Navy's small ships, backed by carrier- and land-based aviation, and fully exploiting the initial advantages of surprise and concentration, would fight for and secure command of the seas and then retain it in a series of actions with growing but fragmented enemy strength.

But as recognition of the material difficulties under which Japan labored increased – and the Imperial Navy if not the more boorish Army was conscious of Japan's marked inability to match potential enemies' numerical strength – the Japanese called upon two further factors to ensure success. To offset numerical weakness the Japanese relied on superior morale and superior quality of equipment. The former was not to show itself to the full until the later stages of the Pacific War. Then, from late 1944 onward, Japan's superior martial and moral resources were mobilized not to secure victory but in an increasingly desperate effort to stave off defeat. This mental fortitude showed itself in the recourse to kamikaze tactics. These tactics were the embodiment of a willingness, even desire, to die in the service of a divine emperor. But the

reliance on superiority of equipment and material was revealed much earlier in the war. From the start of the conflict the superior quality of Japanese equipment – in battleships, aircraft carriers, cruisers, destroyers, torpedoes, shells, pyrotechnics, searchlights and particularly aircraft – was very quickly evident, to the surprise and discomfort of Japan's enemies. In no case was this more so than with the Zero-sen.

The Zero was the best-known and longest-serving Japanese aircraft of World War II. In production right up until the end of the conflict, the Zero was also the most numerous of Japan's aircraft, though the precise number built can never be known because of the destruction of records caused by American bombing in the last year of the war. The Zero was to Japan what the Spitfire was to Britain and the B-17 was to the United States of America. All were superb aircraft and were symbols of nations at war. Indeed, such was the longevity of the Zero that her very name is all but identical with the term 'Japanese air power.' But she differed from the Spitfire or the B-17 as from any other aircraft of the other combatant powers in that she was never forced to share the limelight nor was she ever eclipsed by any other aircraft in the national armory. Both in victory and adversity the spearhead of Japanese air power was the Zero, and herein the aircraft reflected the story of Japan

Below: Although it was regarded as cheap and expendable, the A6M2's simplicity and gracefulness is clearly captured in this photograph.

Above: **Training Zero pilots on Penang Island off Malaya during the summer of 1942.**

and the Imperial Navy in the course of the Pacific War. In the early months of conflict a superbly trained and equipped Japanese war machine, with the Zero in the van, stormed through Southeast Asia, annihilating ill-co-ordinated British, Dutch and American efforts to stem a seemingly irresistible flood. In those days for any Allied aircraft to take to the air to do battle with the Zero was tantamount to an act of suicide on the part of its pilot. Initially no Allied aircraft could live with the Zero whose qualities had been unanticipated and unappreciated by Allied intelligence staffs before the war. (The Grumman F4F Wildcat, an American fighter, was able to offer battle and occasionally did not come off second best. But for the first six months of the war the Zero was devastatingly successful and it was not until the latter part of 1942 that certain of the Zero's basic weaknesses were fully appreciated by the Americans. These weaknesses, when tied in with certain advantages the Wildcat was known to have over the Zero, began to be applied tactically toward the end of 1942 and contributed to the decline in Japanese air supremacy.)

Yet as the war progressed Japan herself and her most famous fighter aircraft showed that unsuspected flaws and weaknesses were present in what had seemed an invincible profile. There was a lack of depth of resources in both. As the weaknesses of the Zero became obvious, it became evident that she was unable to match the qualitative and quantative improvements of successive American aircraft. Suitable replacements were sought. As early as 1939 under the terms of the 14-Shi program the Imperial Navy sought a replacement for the Zero. This was to be the J2M. In 1942, under the 17-Shi, the Navy ordered the A7M. Neither of these aircraft, however, reached front-line units in worthwhile numbers; both

Above: **A captured Zero of the A6M5 variety showing her sleek lines and long-barrelled 20mm cannon to full effect.**
Right: **(both): Close-ups of the Zero A6M5 Model 52.**

appeared in prototype and in service between 1942 and 1944, but in totally inadequate strength. Urgent attempts were made to improve the Zero, but its obsolescence was evident even as early as 1943. Although it fought in every theater of operations and in every major action from the Bismarcks, the battles of the Philippine Sea and Leyte Gulf to the last desperate battles over the off-shore islands and the Japanese homeland itself, the Zero always operated on a diminishing scale of effectiveness.

For the purposes of clarification, it is as well to give at this point a list of the various types of Zero that were produced and to explain the rather complicated series of numbering and lettering used by the Imperial Navy for their aircraft. The Zero's correct designation was the A6M. She was ordered under the 12-Shi program and was officially defined as the Naval Type 0 Carrier Fighter. The term 12-Shi means the twelfth year of the reign of the Emperor, Hirohito, who became Emperor in 1926. The Type 0 label stemmed from the fact that the aircraft entered service (or was accepted for service) in what was to the Japanese the year 2600. This corresponds to 1940. Type 96, an immediate predecessor to the Zero, was an aircraft available in and after 1936. (In fact the Zero's predecessor first saw combat in 1937.) The A6M designated the type and manufacturer of the aircraft. The first letter represented the type of aircraft, in this case the A meaning that it was an aircraft designed to operate from a carrier. The second letter indicated the maker, in this case Mitsubishi, while the intervening number indicated the aircraft's place in the list of such types built by that firm. Thus A6M meant that the aircraft was Mitsubishi's sixth aircraft built for carrier operations. A subsequent number showed the Mark of aircraft. The aircraft with which Japan went to war – the most famous of the Zeros – was the A6M2, the

Above: **An A6M2 Model 21 with flaps down and undercarriage extended. This was the aircraft that spearheaded the Japanese air attack during the first year of the war.**

second Mark of Zero ever produced. Subsequently there could be either numbers, small letters or capital letters to indicate the specialist characteristics of an aircraft. The use of the suffix -N, for example, indicated a basic aircraft modified for amphibious work. The A6M2-N was a basic Zero with floats. The A6M2-K was a two-seater trainer. Various designations will be explained in the course of the text. It is as well to remember that the official name of the aircraft was the Reisen, and the official Allied codename (subject to much confusion) was the Zeke. In order of appearance the list of major Zero variants was as follows:

A6M1 – the prototypes	
A6M2 – Naval Type 0 Carrier Fighter	
	Model 11
	(This is the full designation)
A6M2	Model 21
A6M3	Model 32
A6M3	Model 22
A6M3	Model 22a
A6M4 – work abandoned on this project with only two prototypes completed.	
A6M5	Model 52
A6M5a, b and c	Models 52a, 52b and 52c respectively
A6M6c	Model 53c
A6M7	Model 63
A6M8c	Model 54c
A6M8	Model 64

In the war the Zero was responsible for conducting a series of rear-guard actions for which it was increasingly ill-suited. The aircraft on which in 1941 so many Japanese hopes had been pinned, proved totally incapable of reversing or even halting Japan's increasingly rapid slide into defeat. Final collapse, of course, cannot be laid at the feet of one aircraft and one service. Japan's defeat in war was a reflection of political, strategic, psychological and materialistic miscalculations. The

wars with China and Russia were wars against weak dynasties more fearful of revolution from within than defeat from without. The Pacific conflict of World War II, on the other hand, was waged against the greatest of the democracies, and was a war that Japan could not limit. Although the Zero in many ways reflected these errors, weaknesses and miscalculations, the achievements of the Zero at the start of the war could not be obscured. For six months this aircraft ruled the skies and helped precipitate political and social upheaval in Southeast Asia, the consequences of which are with us to this day.

The origins of the Zero are to be found in circumstances peculiar to Japan's situation in the 1920s and early 1930s. Japanese concepts of war, command of the seas and the role of individual parts of her armed forces have already been mentioned. Within these concepts it must be stressed that the evolution of the Zero was deliberate and systematic in that it fulfilled a basic need for a fast, highly maneuverable attack aircraft capable of operating over long ranges in the vastness of the Pacific Ocean. The Zero and other outstanding aircraft also owed their origins to the new concepts of naval warfare pioneered by such men as Rear Admiral Isoroku Yamamoto who focused his attention on that revolutionary instrument of navies, the aircraft carrier, then in its infancy.

Moreover, the development of the Zero must be seen in the context of Japan's emergence to self-reliance with regard to armaments, and her break with her dependence on Western technology. This process had been underway for some time before the gestation of the Zero, but it can be argued, with much force, that the Zero really marked the point where Japan ceased to be an imitative nation and showed herself capable of building high-technology weapons superior to those of her former mentors. Admittedly, the Zero was designed and built by men some of whom had studied or trained

Above: An A6M5 Model 52 is refuelled from a barrel. Note the 20mm cannon.
Below: The Zeros were the guardians of Japan's conquests: A6M3 Zeros lined up on Bougainville in early 1943 during the Guadalcanal campaign.

abroad, but the aircraft was an all-Japanese, high-quality product. Thus it was the evolution of the Japanese Naval Air Service, its initial work with carriers and the attitudes of such aviation fanatics as Yamamoto that were at the root of aircraft development.

Japanese naval aviation was new, of course. In 1912 the Imperial Navy created the Naval Aeronautical Research Committee and sent six officers to France and the United States of America to learn to fly. The activities of these officers also included learning to maintain and service aircraft and they were charged with securing aircraft for service in Japan. When the six returned in late 1912 they brought with them aircraft from Henri Farman and from Curtiss. These aircraft were operated after November 1912 from the Yokosuka Naval Air Station. Very quickly, learning as they went along and from other nations, the Japanese passed a series of milestones in the development of the Japanese Naval Air Service. In 1913 a seaplane tender, the *Wakamaiya Maru*, was built; in 1914 Japanese aircraft gained the honor of being the first aircraft in the world to sink an enemy warship, albeit an auxiliary minelayer of minimal fighting value, in the port of Tsingtao. Between 1916 and 1918 the Navy established two Air Corps on Sasebo and Yokosuka, while in 1917 the first all-Japanese-built and designed naval aircraft was completed. In fact the latter proved to be something of a flash in the pan because Japan at that time was still heavily dependent on Western (particularly British) technical knowledge.

But Japan was very interested in one British development pioneered during World War I. She watched closely Britain's first attempts to experiment with the launching and recovery of aircraft from a moving ship and, independently of Britain,

Above: The pride of the Japanese naval aviation of the prewar period: the *Akagi* in 1941. Refitted in the 1930s with a full-length flight deck, she was one of the largest carriers in the world and served as the flagship of the Pearl Harbor Strike Force.

Left: The spacing between the wheels of the Zero was 3.5m which was wider than its predecessor the Navy Type 96 A5M1.
Right and right below: Zero Model 52 in flight.

came to the conclusion that the only way that aircraft could be satisfactorily handled on a ship was by the incorporation of a continuous free deck, cleared of any obstacle, running the greater part of the length of the ship. In fact by launching the *Hosho* on 13 November 1921 the Japanese for a time led the world in naval aviation because this ship was the first one conceived, designed and built as an aircraft carrier, complete with an unobstructed flight deck. She predated the Royal Navy's *Argus* by several months.

Nevertheless, at the very time that the Japanese were branching out on their own with regard to carriers, their overall reliance on the West was underlined by the fact that they required British help in the form of a semiofficial Naval Mission to reorganize the Aviation Service and to train pilots. The Japanese also recruited Herbert Smith, the ex-chief designer of the Sopwith Aviation Company, to produce a series of aircraft to replace the Sopwith Pup and various other aircraft with which the Japanese were then equipped.

A very abstract idea of aircraft such as the Zero began to enter the picture in 1931 in that certain basic decisions were made regarding the future of Japanese naval aviation. In large part these decisions were made by Yamamoto, but only with the full consent and endorsement of the Navy's hierarchy. Most fundamental was the decision to end any form of reliance upon or association with foreign aviation. Yamamoto wanted a fully contained, self-sufficient Japanese aviation industry, and by that time, 1931, this was within Japan's grasp. The three great aviation companies of Japan – Mitsubishi, Kawasaki and Nakajima – were well established and powerfully backed by the government. The number of home-produced and foreign-trained designers and engineers allowed Japan for the first time in her aviation history to dispense with foreign help. Foreign aircraft were still ordered for evaluation purposes, but no longer for front-line service. Moreover, as time was to show, Yamamoto was formulating certain specific ideas about the functions of naval aviation. He was one of the most perceptive officers in any navy in recognizing the inherently offensive nature of naval aviation. Much of the theory and practice of naval aviation throughout the world at this time was directed toward reconnaissance, defense, spotting for guns and, just occasionally, attacks on an enemy in flight.

Yamamoto, ahead of his time, was considering naval aviation not so much as an adjunct to the big gun but as an independent arm, fighting for and securing air and sea supremacy far beyond the range of naval artillery. Yamamoto was one of the first to realize that the question of which side held control of the air was likely to resolve the question of who possessed command of the seas long before any contact occurred between surface vessels. To realize these new ideas Yamamoto was urging the use of specialized aircraft for specific tasks: he did not favor the development of multirole combat aircraft which, though cheaper than specialized aircraft, were incapable of carrying out any single function effectively. As head of the technical and procurement branch of the Navy in 1931 and one of the very few senior officers in any navy with pilot's wings, Yamamoto was in a good position to put at least some of his ideas into effect. Two matters, far beyond his power, however, served to add urgency to the situation and to help fulfill his objectives.

Left: The first purpose-built carrier *Hosho* in 1923 showing the island superstructure which was later removed.
Right: Isoroku Yamamoto, the architect of the Pearl Harbor operation.

Above: **A forerunner of the Zero, the A4N1 Navy Type 95 biplane was built by Nakajima. It filled the gap caused by the failure of the 7-Shi monoplane fighter but was obsolete by 1941.**

The first was the initial failure of Japanese industry to meet the demands of April 1932 when the Naval Staff began an ambitious program of re-equipment under the terms of the 7-Shi (ie, 1932) program. The Navy ordered two types of monoplane fighter, one from Mitsubishi (a low-winged variant) and the other from Nakajima (a high-wing parasol version). The end products were nothing short of aeronautical disasters, and the Navy was forced to revert to a Nakajima biplane as a stopgap until a more reliable monoplane became available. But the important point was that by the 1930s, despite the inevitable false starts, aviation was moving into the age of the monoplane. While lacking the extreme agility of the biplane, the monoplane possessed certain major characteristics such as higher speed, greater range and offensive power that not only more than offset any advantages the biplane might retain, but

made possible the whole concept of deep penetration raids by naval aircraft. It also made the development of highly specialized aircraft possible, something not always feasible with biplanes. These improvements were to be absolutely essential to the evolution of the A6M.

The second matter that 'hurried' the development of the Navy's program was the ever-deepening Japanese involvement in China after 1931. In that year the mutinous Army overran Manchuria and subsequently began to encroach upon northern China. When full-scale war eventually came in 1937, it became the final link in the chain that led to the production of the Mitsubishi Zero-sen. The 1932 monoplane fiasco had led to the reversion to biplanes. However, by 1934 the Imperial Navy in its 9-Shi program again called for a new single-seater monoplane fighter. The specifications demanded by the Navy were not exacting by its usual standards. There was no demand for an aircraft capable of operating from a carrier, and this allowed the development of a formidable aircraft whose capability of being operated from carriers was a bonus. Specifications required a 217mph speed at 10,000ft, a climb to 16,500ft in 6.5 minutes, dimensions not greater than 11m by 8m (11m being the maximum dimension of elevators on Japanese aircraft carriers) and an armament of two 7.7mm machine guns. Mitsubishi, with its 7-Shi design team still intact but now under the direction of an outstanding designer and engineer, Jiro Horikoshi, replaced its previous disaster with the A5M (Allied codename 'Claude'). This was a low-wing, inverted gull monoplane with a fixed undercarriage. To aid streamlining in order to secure maximum performance, a very small cross-section – and hence engine – was adopted, and the aircraft was given flush-riveted aluminum stressed-skin covering. In fact the A5M surpassed all the desired specifi-

Below: **The A5M2b Naval Type 96 Model 2-2. This is an unusual photograph showing the Claude with an enclosed cockpit and a 20mm cannon mounted above the engine.**

cations by considerable margins. She could make 280mph at 10,500ft and could climb to 16,400ft in less than six minutes. In almost every way the Claude was a match for any fighter in the world at that time, a fact quickly acknowledged with the outbreak of the war in China.

From the start of the conflict the Imperial Navy was involved, intent on using China as a test bed for its tactics with level and dive bombers. The initial results were disastrous, not so much because of any shortcomings on the part of the tactics and the bombers themselves, but because Chinese fighters could shoot the Japanese bombers out of the skies with ease. Even when the Japanese escorted their bombers with the obsolescent A2N1 and A4N1 biplanes, Chinese fighters could operate with impunity. With the bombers hopelessly vulnerable, the A5M was rushed into production and sent to China where it caused a dramatic and immediate transformation on the battlefield. The appearance of the Claude resulted in a veritable slaughter of Chinese fighter aircraft, the A5M quickly establishing not simply a massive material but also a profound psychological superiority over the Chinese Air Force. But good though the Claude undoubtedly was, it had one major weakness as far as the Imperial Navy was concerned. Its radius of action was about 350 miles, and this precluded deep penetration raids either over China or across the wastes of the Pacific.

Even before the Claude was blooded for the first time over Nanking on 18 September 1937, the Imperial Navy had submitted specifications for a 12-Shi carrier fighter to both Mitsubishi and Nakajima. In large measure the Navy's demands for a 12-Shi fighter stemmed from the desire to extend the range of the Claude. In fact, the fighter the Navy sought to acquire by its paper of 19 May 1937 was a replacement for the Claude even before that aircraft had entered combat. But the original specifications, already stringent, were tightened up still further in October 1937 as the first combat evaluation of the A5M was begun. The final, almost crippling demands of the Imperial Navy were for a single-seater monoplane capable of over 310mph in level flight at over 13,000ft, a climb rate of 10,000ft in 3.5 minutes (a twelve percent increase in performance over the Claude), and an endurance of up to two hours at normal cruising speed or up to eight hours at economical cruising speed (about 200mph) when equipped with drop tanks. This aircraft was to carry two 20mm cannon in addition to the two 7.7mm machine guns of the Claude, and had to have provisions for 120kg (264lb) of bombs. The new aircraft had to possess a degree of mobility and maneuverability equivalent to that of the A5M. To these stringent requirements was added the natural demand for a full radio set (the Type 96-Ku-1) and direction finding equipment (the Kiuisi Type Ku-3). Both were absolutely essential if the aircraft was to operate to a range of 800 miles across water, but the most killing provisions of all were the Imperial Navy's demands that the aircraft be able to take off in less than 70m, given a 27-knot headwind. Landing speeds had to be less than 67mph. Not surprisingly the Japanese design teams confronted with these specifications were aghast at the Navy's demands. By any criteria the demands of the Navy were far in excess of anything built hitherto in Japan or in the world. In effect the specifications demanded a carrier aircraft with all the pedigree of a thoroughbred land-based fighter. This was precisely what the Navy wanted. In its demands on armament, agility and endurance, the Imperial Navy was insisting on a naval aircraft vastly superior to most, if not all, land-based fighters belonging to any nation with which Japan might find herself at war in the next few years.

Nakajima decided that the Navy's demands were im-

possible, and the firm had no intention of squandering resources on a project in which it had no real confidence. Nakajima told the Imperial Navy that its demands could not be met. Mitsubishi was hesitant, partly because it was already working on a medium bomber, partly because it was quite aware of the technical problems that would be involved in trying to meet the Imperial Navy's specifications. But Mitsubishi had two clear advantages when it considered the Navy's requirements. Firstly, there was no competition. Secondly, Jiro Horikoshi and his A5M team was not merely still intact but it had been strengthened over the last few years. With this team Mitsubishi decided to attempt to meet the Navy's demands.

From the start of his work Horikoshi set down a three-year timetable for design, testing and production. He allotted one complete year to design, six months for the construction of the prototype, and a full year for trials and evaluation. Subsequently he allowed six months for an initial production run and subsequent testing. This program never progressed as Horikoshi intended: the demands of the China War were such that the first Zeros were committed to combat long before their full trials were completed. In fact, combat came to be part of the testing process. Horikoshi's initial designs and estimates were placed before and accepted by the Naval Board in April 1938; by the summer the first work was being started on the construction of the prototype with parts being cut to Horikoshi's specifications. Mitsubishi worked quickly and completed the first prototype in March 1939, less than a year after the Navy first laid down its demands for the new aircraft.

Horikoshi had a very able team. Most of the mathematical calculations were done by Teruo Tojo and Horikoshi himself, while work on the engine was entrusted to Denichiro Inouye and Shotaro Tanaka. The undercarriage arrangements were the responsibility of Takeyoshi Moror and Sadahiko Kato, while the problems surrounding the new and revolutionary heavy armament were left to Yoshimi Hatakenaka. Hatakenaka's idea to mount the two 7.7mm machine guns on the upper fuselage nose, with synchronized firing through the propeller disk, had two immediate repercussions on the design. Firstly, because the aircraft had to be a strong and stable gun platform, the whole of the nose had to be made longer. Secondly, the whole of the wing assembly had to be extremely strong in order to house the heavy cannon and in order to withstand the strains imposed when firing the heavy cannon either during a climb or a dive. The solution to having such heavy weights outside the propeller disk was to build the wing spar as an integral part of the fuselage to spread the dead weight. The wing, apart from the spar, was made as one intact piece. Behind these developments was another equally important consideration. The wing had to be strong, but it also had to be light. By building the wing as a complete unit and the wing spar as part of the fuselage, Mitsubishi cut down to a bare minimum the number of heavy fasteners and connectors needed to hold the aircraft together. This saved more than 100lb in weight. Dispensing with normally-accepted practices in such matters was of vital importance in design considerations. If the Zero was to attain the same high level of maneuverability as the A5M, she had to combine strength with extreme lightness, a large expanse of wing area, long span ailerons and exceptionally lean lines. Every possible weight-saving device was used, including the first extensive use of a new substance, Extra Super-Duralumin, in the airframe and spar caps. To further save weight the wings were covered with fabric, not metal. In addition, of course, the small cross-section and engine that had been incorporated into the Claude were worked into the new design. Hirokoshi

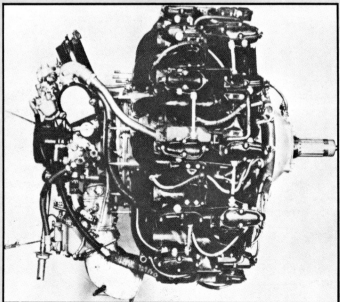

used the Mitsubishi Mark 2 Zuisei 13 engine as his powerpack. This was a 14-cylinder twin-row radial engine of 780hp, with an emergency rating of 875hp. It was a very compact and well-streamlined engine, but from the start it never really proved satisfactory.

Its initial problems stemmed from the fact that it was equipped, on the insistence of the Naval Board, with a twin-bladed variable pitch airscrew, but the Sumitomo-Hamilton propeller had to be abandoned in the course of trials in favor of a three-blade, paddle-bladed, constant-speed propeller. The whole of the engine gave problems, and the technical difficulties encountered during the design and prototype construction phase were not eased by disputes within the Imperial Navy over the relative merits of speed and endurance on the one hand, and maneuverability on the other. At every stage in development emphasis was placed on extreme agility, but there were many who wondered whether this agility was obtained at too high a price in terms of speed and endurance. Lieutenant Commander Shibata, one of the foremost Naval pilots and commander of the training school, was one who felt this way. He was prepared to accept less agility – which he considered could be compensated for by the extreme thoroughness of the Navy's pilot training programs – in return for range and speed. These he considered far more vital than tight turning in a dogfight, in the context of the vast distances involved in the theaters of operation where Japan fought. He reasoned that Japanese aircraft simply could not afford to lose a contact with an enemy on account of inferiority of speed or range.

While there was much to recommend Shibata's line of argument, he lost out in the round of discussions, mainly because Mitsubishi was adamant that Shibata's aircraft would prove markedly inferior in overall performance to the aircraft

Above left: **The Nakajima Sakae 21 (NK1F) later known as the (Ha-35) 21 powered the A6M5.**
Left: **The Sakae 12 (NK1C), which later became the (Ha-35) 12, powered the A6M2 and could achieve up to 940 hp.**

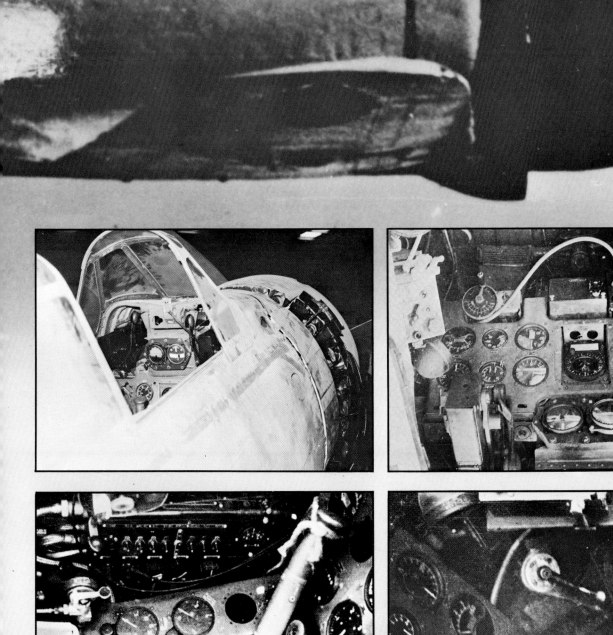

Below: A Zero A6M3.
Bottom: Close-ups of the Zero cockpit. Note the 7.7mm Type 97 machine guns in the upper fuselage.

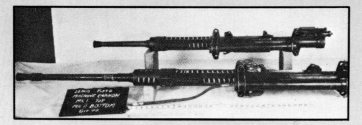

Above: The 20mm Type 99 Model 2 Mark 3 cannon (below) and the 20mm Type 99 Model 1 Mark 3 cannon.

already being developed. Most combat pilots supported Mitsubishi. Prevailing opinion among the pilots was strongly in favor of nimbleness in order to get in the first devastating burst of heavy fire on enemy aircraft. Mitsubishi and the pilots accepted that the price for high maneuverability had to be paid for in relatively poor handling characteristics at extreme altitude and an inability to either outdive or to outroll stronger Western aircraft. Under certain conditions the Zero could be sluggish. This was unfortunate, but accepted as thus. Little real store was set on these weaknesses which, in any case, were partially offset by subsequent developments. More serious than this, however, was the one basic weakness that the Zero incorporated in order to obtain the amazing degree of maneuverability the pilots demanded. The lightness of the aircraft was obtained in large part by robbing it of inherent strength and robustness, and, most critically, by the deliberate refusal to incorporate armor protection for the pilot and to provide self-sealing fuel tanks. Such devices, then becoming standard in aircraft in Western countries, were scorned by Japanese pilots.

With the whole of the philosophy of the Zero dedicated to the fast-attack fighter for use in offensive operations, there was little patience for passive means of protection that merely added dead weight to aircraft. As a consequence the Zero was scarcely airworthy by Western standards, but by Japanese standards she was just what was required. With no armor, lightness of airframe and lack of heavy fittings, the prototype Zero weighed 4380lb, compared to the prototype Spitfire's 5332lb. It was a price that the Japanese felt was worth paying, but ultimately the long-term cost of such arrangements was found to be very heavy. Without proper drop tanks in many cases – some were even made of plywood – and self-sealing tanks, the Zero was vulnerable to flame; while the lack of armor protection behind the pilot caused him to be needlessly exposed. Moreover, the Zero tended to crumple quickly when caught in a burst of fire because of its lack of structural strength and rigidity.

Some time elapsed before these weaknesses became apparent, but they did limit the effectiveness of the Zero in a defensive role. This, after all, was crucial as far as the Japanese were concerned. Once they had secured their initial objectives, the Japanese had to assume defensive tactics. When utilizing surprise and concentration the Zero was a superb fighter for securing air supremacy in accordance with the first phase of the Japanese plan of operations in the Pacific War. But those very qualities that made the aircraft so formidable in the attack were obtained at a price that left the Zero fatally

Right: By 1944 American industry had produced overwhelming numbers of ships and aircraft. The *Leyte* (CV.32) and seventeen escort carriers in reserve at the end of the war.
Below: Outnumbering even automobiles F6F Hellcats on the asphalt.

weak when it came to facing the prolonged battle of wearing down enemy resolve. This was unappreciated by most of the Navy at the time, but in the long run these weaknesses proved to be the aircraft's Achilles' heel.

It is appropriate to consider two further weaknesses of the Zero that became increasingly evident. These weaknesses, as they became manifest in the course of the Pacific War, were important in that they affected significantly the fortunes of the A6M in combat. Firstly, it must be stressed that the Zero was an extremely difficult aircraft to build. It was costly in its demands on skilled labor, which was short, and extremely expensive in terms of the time taken to build individual units. The extremely low level of productivity stemmed from the fact that the Zero was built as a single-unit machine. The process whereby the fuselage and wing spar were built as one and the whole of the wing was built as a single item prevented the development of mass-production techniques. It was im-

possible for the Japanese to produce individual parts *en masse* from a whole variety of manufacturing centers and then to assemble the aircraft at one central point where all those parts could be brought together. The aircraft had to be laboriously and painstakingly built *in situ*, taking up desperately needed factory space.

Despite the fact that the Japanese aircraft industry showed massive increases in production between 1941 and 1944, and even allowing for the fact that the Zero was the most numerous of Japan's aircraft, the slowness of construction, the high cost of individually produced aircraft and the drain imposed on the labor force served to frustrate the rapid build-up of strength in 1942 and 1943 when more aircraft were urgently required. Japanese aircraft production rose 74 percent in 1942 over the 1941 total, and then by 88 percent and 69 percent in successive years. In that time production rose from 5088 aircraft a year to 28,180, but it was only in 1944 that

Below: **A captured Zero A6M5 fighter which has been roughly painted back to its Japanese markings.**

Japanese aircraft production passed the American 1941 production level. Even in that year the Japanese were building one for every four that the American factories produced. With regard to fighter aircraft the situation was even worse for Japan. Only in 1944 did fighter production pass the 10,000 per year mark. The great increase in aircraft production therefore served not to consolidate success but to reinforce failure; it came too late to be effective. Even allowing for the smallness of Japan's industrial base, the natural disasters she faced such as the earthquake of 7 December 1944 that severely damaged the Nagoya works, and the manmade problems that affected production (loss of labor to the services, loss of raw materials as a result of merchant shipping sinkings, bombing raids), the fact remains that the design of the Zero was not conducive to speedy construction.

The other weakness that dogged the performance of the Zero in the middle and later stages of the Pacific War was the declining ability of Japanese pilots. The training schools were totally inadequate to train pilots either in numbers or in intensity at a rate that would cover the 'wastage' that is inevitable and extremely high in modern war. Even in the period of success Japanese air losses were not light, but they were among the best of the pilots. These pilots were hardened veterans of the China War who were irreplaceable. In the hands of an experienced pilot the weaknesses of the Zero were not too important because Allied aircraft seldom had the chance to get in a telling burst of fire on the jinking A6M. Even before the Battle of the Coral Sea in May 1942 the Commander in Chief of the Combined Fleet, Yamamoto, was warned of the declining standard of Japanese air crew. As the war progressed pilot inexperience and Zero frailties fed off one another. By 1943 the Zero was dated: in the hands of poorly trained pilots the aircraft that had been ruler of the skies for a brief period became little more than a death trap.

THE A6M1 AND A6M2

Work on the prototype A6M1 at Mitsubishi's Nagoya works was completed in the course of March 1939, the aircraft being wheeled out for the first time on the 19th. Her departure for trials was more than a little ignominious for an aircraft supposedly better than anything else in existence. She had to be towed secretly by ox-wagon to the neighboring Army airfield at Kagamigahara for her trials. Her first major ground tests and flight took place on 1 April when she was taken into the air by Mitsubishi's chief test pilot, Katsuzo Shima. From the first the A6M1 encountered problems, but they were mainly of a minor nature. The braking system proved inadequate while the oil temperature rose alarmingly on even the shortest of flights. She also suffered from being underpowered and from severe vibration, but this was corrected by the change of propeller. The A6M1 was able to meet all the Navy's specifications but one; she could not make her designed speed, and was capable of only (sic) 300mph. But after 162 flying hours the first of the two prototypes was accepted by the Imperial Navy on 14 September. The second prototype was accepted from Mitsubishi on 25 October. These were the only true prototypes of the Zero ever built by Mitsubishi.

The Imperial Navy was impressed by the A6M1 but gave orders for the third and subsequent models to be fitted with the 940/950hp Nakajima Sakae (meaning 'prosperity') 12 engine. These aircraft, which came to be designated the A6M2 Naval Type 0 Carrier Aircraft Model 11, had various minor modifications from the original prototypes, most notably in the strengthening of the undercarriage, brakes and wing spars. The first of the Model 11s made its maiden flight on 28 December 1939.

The initial trials of both Marks lasted until July 1940 when the Navy accepted fifteen preproduction models of the A6M2 for service. The Imperial Navy found that many of the initial faults had been eliminated in the course of testing and production. The new engine gave the Zero a top speed of about 330mph at 16,000ft and she was found to be a very easy aircraft to fly with excellent all-round vision for the pilot. Various minor problems that arose were met by in-production modifications. From the twenty-second production model onward the rear wing span was strongly reinforced, mainly because it was believed that control flutter had caused the second A6M1 to suffer excessive vibration during a dive that led to the loss of both pilot and aircraft in an accident on 11 March 1940. From the one hundred and ninety-second production model onward modified aileron tabs were incorporated to enhance maneuverability at lower altitudes, while from the sixty-fifth onward the A6M2 incorporated manually-folding wing tips that allowed the aircraft to fit the elevators of the carriers. Aircraft with this capability were designated the Model 21. The Model 11 and the Model 21 in fact showed no real differences and in the years 1940 and 1941 were effectively the only models of the A6M2 in existence. It was the A6M2 that carried the weight of the Japanese air onslaught in the first year of the war, but thereafter it was phased out of frontline duties though various modifications allowed it to be used for a variety of specialized functions. These functions included antisubmarine patrolling, reconnaissance, training and, inevitably toward the end of the war, kamikaze attacks.

The testing of the A6M2 had to be compressed because of the Imperial Navy's demands for Zeros to support operations

Above: Two Zeros on patrol together, both Model 21s.
Below: An A6M2 of the 12th Rengo Kokutai, one of the first to see service.

Above: Fourth from the left, Major General Claire Chennault, the commander of American 'volunteers' in China.

in China. Beginning in May 1940 the Navy began to deploy the first of the preproduction Model 11s to China where bomber losses had started to rise again as the Japanese began to mount long-distance bombing raids beyond the range of the Claude and Army fighters. By the end of July the Imperial Navy had concentrated its fifteen A6M2 Model 11s with the 12th Combined Naval Air Corps – and, significantly, had started trials with the Model 21 on the carrier *Kaga*. The aircraft allotted to the 12th had not been fully tested, but the Navy was confident that the Zero would not only perform well but that any further problems could be resolved on the spot. Apart from fuel vaporization which was cured by recourse to a higher octane fuel, no such difficulties arose. Because the aircraft had withstood forces greater than 5G in the course of its trials there was good reason for the Navy to be confident that the Zero could deal with any fighter that China put into the air.

Above: **Zero-sen fighters on a combat mission over mainland China prior to the outbreak of World War II.**

On 19 August 1940 the Zero flew its first combat mission. Twelve A6M2 Model 11s escorted a fifty-bomber raid on Chungking, the then-capital of Nationalist China. The Chinese fighters declined battle on this and subsequent occasions, and it was not until 13 September – at roughly the same time that new production models were having their wing spans strengthened – that the Zero drew blood for the first time. On that day Chinese fighters, having been dispersed when warned of the forthcoming attack, again declined to give battle over Chungking. Thirty minutes after the bombers had ended their runs and had turned for their bases, the Zeros reappeared over Chungking's airfields in time to catch the returning Chinese fighters for whom the danger seemed to have passed. In the course of a wild melee that lasted the whole of thirty minutes, all 27 Chinese fighters (mainly biplanes and monoplanes of Soviet manufacture) were destroyed for no loss among the Zeros. The Japanese, however, were only able to claim 22 kills because three Chinese aircraft had been abandoned in the air by their pilots at the first sign of trouble and two others suffered a midair collision. In the weeks that followed roughly the same story was repeated at various cities. In October the Zeros accounted for nineteen Chinese aircraft at Chengtu and it was over this city, on 14 March 1941, that one of the very rare major air actions of the Sino–Japanese war took place. In this action the Zeros accounted for 24 Chinese fighters, again at no cost to themselves. Such success, however, was rare because by 1941 there was very little left of the Chinese air force (despite unofficial American support) and that which remained constantly evaded battle. In the course of its operations over Chinese territory the A6M2s accounted for 99 Chinese aircraft and secured total command of the skies. By its success the Zero allowed Japanese bombers free range over Chinese cities, and this was achieved at the cost of precisely two Zeros. Neither was lost in air combat; both were brought down by ground fire, the first operational loss being in May 1941. Great though the victory had been, it had been achieved at the cost of loss of security. Western observers in China (and Japan), and the French in Indo-China, noted the appearance of a new fighter with exceptional range and powers of maneuver. From combat reports and sketches a very accurate summary of the Zero's main characteristics had been drawn up for the British and American governments. Moreover, the commander of the American 'volunteers' in China, Claire Chennault, had even devised tactics to try to deal with the Zero. Fortunately for the Japanese, however, reports of a 'super-fighter' were discounted in Washington and London. The Royal Air Force in Singapore was scathingly disdainful of reports on the Zero. The Japanese air forces were dismissed as being of decidedly inferior quality at a time when all the facts pointed in quite the opposite direction. It was firmly believed in Singapore that the Brewster F2-A Buffalo, a not particularly impressive aircraft at the best of times, could be relied upon to look after the British position and interests in the Far East. It was openly stated that Spitfires and Hurricanes were not needed in the defense of Malaya and India. Thus were the Japanese aided even by their enemies, and from September 1941 onward the Japanese Naval Air Force began to redeploy its strength toward the Pacific and Southeast Asia for what was then the inevitable conflict with the Western Powers.

At the outbreak of the Pacific War 328 of the 521 fighters carried by Japanese aircraft carriers were A6M2 Model 21s. In time all Japanese carriers were to convert fully to A6M2s. Most of the first-line land-based flotillas had Zeros as their cutting edge, but here the Japanese faced serious problems. With not many more Zeros available for their land-based forces than for the carriers, the Navy had to come to terms with operating over a much greater area than the carriers and with a much diluted strength. The Japanese were forced to work to margins of error that were precariously narrow even by their own standards. Naturally the strength of the land-based Zeros was directed against two targets – the British in Malaya and the Americans in the Philippines. These were the obvious targets because they were the only two forces standing between Japan and the conquest of the whole of Southeast Asia. In effect only the Americans offered a real challenge to the Japanese quest for mastery of the western Pacific, and only the Zero had the range to escort bombers from Japanese bases on Formosa to their objectives (American airfields) in central Luzon.

It has been recounted that in the opening months of the war Japanese forces swiftly overran their opponents, inflicting on them a series of massive, humiliating defeats. In the vanguard of conquest was the Zero. In operations stretching over 125 degrees of longitude, from Pearl Harbor via the islands of the southwest Pacific, Darwin, greater Indo-China and Burma to Ceylon, the Zero met and defeated each Allied challenge it faced. From the start of the campaign the more perceptive observer would have recognized certain danger signals to be read into events even in the midst of victory. Over Pearl Harbor the Japanese had lost nine Zeros. Anticipated losses had been much higher, but it was significant that one raid over American territory cost the Japanese more than four times as many fighter aircraft as had been lost over China in more than twelve months of combat.

In the raids over the Indian Ocean the Zero encountered Martlets and Hurricanes. Losses were relatively light, success was great. The going was getting harder, and there was no comfort to be drawn from the experience of the Battle of the Coral Sea. This battle in May 1942 was the first naval battle fought entirely by carrier aircraft. The Japanese lost heavily in terms of pilots and aircraft and their carriers were so extensively damaged that they were unavailable for the next

The Zero was in the van of Japanese conquests in the first six months of the war. The Pearl Harbor attack was spearheaded by Zeros and Val dive bombers which shattered enemy aircraft and anti-aircraft positions before the main bombers came in.
Left: US Army fighters and hangars on Wheeler Field, 7 December 1941.
Below left: Bombers on Hickam Field blaze in their hangars.
Below: The first Zero to be captured by the Americans in the Pearl Harbor attack. American intelligence got its first though incomplete look at a Zero at close quarters.
Bottom: The crew cheer as a Kate torpedo bomber takes off from a Japanese carrier to follow up the damage inflicted by the Zeros.

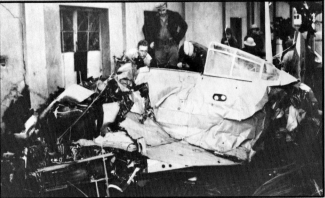

from below and from the rear because they had a poor regard for the ventral defenses of the Allied Fortress; they also realized that the early versions of the B-17 had no rear turret. The poorly defended tail section of the Flying Fortress invited attack, and the Japanese Zero duly obliged. Subsequently, with the appearance of the B-17E, complete with rear turret and power-operated dorsal turret, the Japanese chose to make head-on attacks against the poorly protected and weakly defended nose before rolling and peeling off in order to present as small a target as possible to the American gunners.

In making such attacks the Japanese were made uncomfortably aware of the power of the B-17's 0.5in (12.7mm) Browning machine guns. The Japanese were forced to recognize their own vulnerability because of the lack of armor protection for the pilot and the absence of self-sealing tanks. As the Japanese quickly became aware of the problems of destroying a B-17, they were forced to recognize certain major offensive weaknesses of the Zero. With only sixty rounds of ammunition for the 20mm cannon and only rifle-sized machine guns, the Zero did not have the firepower to deal with a B-17 properly. In Europe the Fortress showed that she could absorb massive damage and still survive; in the Pacific the Japanese were made aware of this fact from an early date. Because of limited oxygen and ammunition supplies the Zero had the ability to make only five or possibly six runs against a B-17, and with closing speeds of 500mph or more, it was difficult to inflict telling damage on a B-17 in the time available before action had to be broken off. Even where shooting accuracy was achieved the Zero suffered from the fact that its ammunition was primed to explode on impact. In a specialist report relating to the problems of attacking B-17s prepared by Lieutenant Commander Kofukuda and Lieutenant Kono in 1942, the two Japanese officers drew the attention of their superiors to the armor and fuel tank weaknesses of the Zero and stressed the need for much greater fire-power.

phase of operations. The initial stages of the Pacific War revealed that although the Zero was superior in all-round performance to any Allied fighter that opposed it, the margin of superiority was extremely small in technical terms, and that in certain respects the Zero was definitely inferior to some of its enemies. Though the relative weakness of the Zero at high altitude, in diving and in rolling had been accepted before the war almost with a state of equanimity, in practice these deficiencies meant that many potential victims escaped destruction by being able to outrun the Zero in a power dive. This was particularly marked in the Allied Wildcat, though the full effect of this discovery was not to be felt until toward the end of 1942.

The lack of internal robustness and strength thus had a hidden price, while combat with airborne B-17s also served to show the Japanese that there were problems with the A6M2. Naturally Japanese fighters opted to attack an airborne B-17

Below: **Zero A6M2s in the Solomons. Note that the censor has removed the unit markings.**

Two American aircraft that met the initial challenge of the Zero:
Opposite top: The F4F Wildcat which was constantly outclassed.
Above: The B-17 Flying Fortress (seen here over California) proved
resistant to Zero attacks.

The Characteristics of the A6M2

Despite minor differences between the Model 11 and the Model 21, the two are considered as one. This aircraft was the original Zero at the start of the Pacific War.

Official Description:
Single-seater, carrier-borne fighter-interceptor. All-metal construction with fabric-covered control surfaces.

Crew:
One pilot in enclosed cockpit. No armor protection.

Dimensions:

Span	12.00m	39ft 4.44in
Length	9.06m	29ft 8.69in
Height	3.05m	10ft 0.06in
Wing Area	22.44sq m	241.54sq ft
Wing Load	107.40kg/sq m	22lb/sq ft

Weights:

Empty	1,680kg	3,704lb
Loaded	2,420kg	5,313lb
Maximum	2,796kg	6,164lb

Powerpack:
One Nakajima NKIC Sakae 12 fourteen-cylinder air-cooled radial engine: 940hp at takeoff; 950hp at 4,200m/13,780ft

Speeds, Ceiling and Rates of Climb:

Maximum	332mph / 534kph	at	5,067m / 16,570ft
Cruising	207mph / 334kph	at	4,012m / 13,120ft
Service Ceiling	10,300m		33,790ft

Maximum Initial rate of climb

in one minute	1,370m	4,500ft
in 7 mins 27 secs	6,000m	19,685ft

(from standing start, no headwind)

Fuel:
With drop tank of 72.6 Imp gallons a total of 156 Imp gallons

Ranges

Normal Range	1,160 miles/1,771km
Long Range	1,930 miles/3,110km

Armament:
Two 7.7mm (0.303in) machine guns, fuselage mounted. 500 rounds per gun.
Two 20mm (0.787in) cannon, wing mounted. Drum fed. 60 rounds per gun.
Wing racks for either two 30kg/66lb or two 60kg/132lb bombs.

Turning Circle:
Radius of turn at 230mph/370kph 1,118ft/340m
Radius at slow combat speed 612ft/186m
Diving 180° turn:
entry speed 230mph/370kph; exit speed 189mph/304kph
Time taken 5.62 seconds

Other factors:
Normal positive-G load factor 7G ⎱ Both cases additional
Normal negative-G load factor 3.5G ⎰ safety factor of 1.8G

Prewar Production

A6M2 prototypes by Mitsubishi: started in Dec 1939		17
A6M2 Model 11 by Mitsubishi: started 31 July 1940		47
A6M2 Model 21 by Mitsubishi: started in Nov 1940		127
by Mitsubishi and Nakajima, with aileron tab modifications, started on 17 April 1941		1,425

Note: Last production figure is an estimate.

Above and left: Views of the A6M2.
Below: DI-108 the A6M2 in which Petty Officer Tadayoshi Koga was killed while attempting to crash land in the Aleutian Islands.

Indeed by the time the Japanese had completed the conquest of Southeast Asia, the effectiveness of the A6M2 was almost at an end, though neither the Japanese nor the Americans could have foreseen this, either in its finality or rapidity. At Midway in June 1941 the elite carrier forces were smashed beyond recall when, in a moment of good fortune, American dive bombers caught the Japanese carriers in the process of rearming and refuelling their aircraft on their decks. With the loss of four fleet carriers and many of the Imperial Navy's best pilots in this battle, the cutting edge of the IJNAF had been decisively blunted, though the Americans were in no position to exploit their victory on a still-powerful enemy. In fact defeat at Midway merely served to reinforce Japanese determination to consolidate their control over the Bismarcks and Solomons, and it was in this area of the Southwest Pacific that the A6M2s fought their last battles as front-line fighters. The last occasion on which the A6M2 Model 21 was used in a major role in a carrier battle was at the Battle of Santa Cruz (26/27 October 1942), but even with the assistance of Zeros based on Rabaul the carrier aircraft proved incapable of securing air supremacy over the disputed island of Guadalcanal for the Japanese.

There were several reasons for the decline of the all-conquering A6M2 in the early part of 1942. The first and most obvious was that Guadalcanal was the first battle where American resources were supplied at a rate faster than those of Japan. The Japanese had always wanted a battle of attrition but not on these terms. At Guadalcanal the Americans held the advantage of position, and from the start the air battle went wrong for the Japanese. It was not a battle they could control: American resources were simply too great for the Japanese to curb.

The second reason for this deteriorating situation related directly to the A6M2 itself. The aircraft was really a 'one-shot' weapon. Rather like blitzkrieg, the first use could prove devastating, the second use could prove very successful, but the third time was courting disaster. The Zero was effective both psychologically and physically, but the real strength of the Zero in 1941–42 was in its potential for concentrated shock and surprise rather than in its physical manifestations, great though these were. To have a carrier fighter capable of outflying land-based aircraft in 1941 was miraculous. For such an aircraft to be Japanese was for white-supremist adversaries nothing short of a shattering experience, but one from which they could recover if given time. The vastness of the Pacific and the limited nature of Japanese war aims provided them with that time, and by late 1942 new American aircraft, the P-38 Lightning, the F4U-1 Corsair and later the Hellcat (and the British Supermarine Spitfire) could match the Zero. Though these aircraft could not match the range and the agility of the A6M2 in a dogfight, their maneuverability was greater than earlier Allied fighters and their firepower and defensive armor were far superior to that of the Zero. By October 1942 the Americans had evolved tactics to try to surpass the Zero.

The evolution of tactics to counter the Zero had come about almost accidentally. In the course of the Aleutian operations that formed part of the Japanese deception plans for the attack on Midway in June 1942, an A6M2 Model 21, flown from the carrier *Ryujo* by Petty Officer Tadayoshi Koga, had been forced to make an emergency landing on a barren island. It seems that Koga mistakenly believed the ground to be firm, but landing in soft soil his aircraft flipped, breaking the pilot's neck. Surprisingly the aircraft was practically undamaged. Sighted by an American reconnaissance aircraft, the wreck was recovered by an American party and then shipped back to

Above: **A later version of the P-38 Lightning, the aircraft credited with more confirmed Zero kills than any other aircraft.**
Right: **The F6F Hellcat was a truly war-winning aircraft which had the edge on the Zero because it had better protection.**

mainland USA for testing. From July onward the Americans subjected their capture to a series of severe trials. They were amazed by the aircraft's construction and lightness, but impressed by what they found. All the weaknesses were probed in weeks of thorough testing and by September a preliminary report of the Zero's capabilities had been issued to combat crews. By 31 October full evaluation reports were available. It was this series of trials and evaluation tests that enabled the Wildcats, Lightnings and Corsairs to adopt the tactics of trying to outdive a Zero before turning sharply in an effort to catch the pursuing but slower Zero with bursts of fire into either the fuel tanks or the unprotected cockpits. American pilots knew that virtually any burst of gunfire into a Zero was likely to destroy it. For these tactics the A6M2 had no effective answer, and the task of trying to meet the challenge posed by new American aircraft and tactics was passed to the A6M3.

Above: A captured A6M3 Model 32 in flight. Note the fuselage-mounted 7.7mm machine guns. Model 32 was codenamed Hamp by Allied intelligence until it was realized that despite its square wing tips the plane was another Zeke version and was codenamed Zeke 32.
Below: An A6M3 Model 22.

THE A6M3

When Kono and Kofukuda made their report stressing the need for greater offensive and defensive power for the Zero, they were not in a position to realize that various measures had already been applied to improve the A6M2. The report does not seem to have received the attention it merited, but the circumstances surrounding the appearance of the A6M3 merely served to reveal the extent to which the Japanese were caught on a self-destructive treadmill by 1942. At this stage of the war Japan needed not merely a new fighter, but many of them. None was forthcoming. The J2M, the replacement for the Zero, was conceived as a land-based interceptor as early as 1938, but it was not until 1942 that the first prototype flew.

Part of the delay can be explained by Horikoshi's divided attention between the A6M and the J2M, but most of the delays revolved around the many problems encountered in J2M production. The worst of the difficulties centered on the Kasei 23a engine, Japan's first engine with water-methanol injection, but there were to be many other difficulties involving all aspects of the aircraft. For Japan the delays were disastrous. It was disastrous because the J2M, a short-ranged but maneuverable aircraft, possessed two assets lacking in the Zero. Armor protection was afforded the pilot while the 7.7mm machine guns were discarded in favor of two more wing-mounted 20mm cannon located beyond the propeller disk. This was the very type of aircraft that Japan needed at this stage of the war because for the first time, the tide of war turned against her. She had to have an aircraft that could hand out and take heavy punishment. Lightweight fragile machines were not what was required, but it was all that the Japanese had available. The Japanese were forced to make do with upgraded versions of the A6M2, but despite their improvements, the new replacements proved as incapable as the A6M2 of stemming the mounting pressure the Americans were beginning to exert. The Japanese were in a desperate position and it was in this hopeless context of mounting and insurmountable odds, that the A6M3 – a totally inadequate weapon – had to make its debut.

The development of the A6M3 had begun long before Kono and his superior officer wrote their report; its development in fact preceded the outbreak of the Pacific War. A full six months before Pearl Harbor Mitsubishi had begun work on an improved Zero. It was inevitable that the emphasis of the work should not have been directed toward the measures that were essential by 1942. With the development of the A6M3, Mitsubishi was still attempting to improve speed and handling characteristics under the direct instructions of the Imperial Navy. As a result, when the A6M3 began to enter service in mid-1942, it was as ill-suited to a defensive battle as its predecessor had been. It had to bear the brunt of the campaign to defend the upper Solomons and the Bismarcks barrier, especially after the collapse of the A6M2 effort in October. It was even less well equipped to meet the strategic and tactical conditions pertaining to the theater than the A6M2.

Top left: Four Betty bombers, Mitsubishi G4Ms, press home an attack at Guadalcanal, August 1942.
Above and Below: A6M3s in Rabaul in 1943. The failure of the new Mark of Zero to achieve results in the battles in the Solomons was in a large part responsible for the abandonment of Guadalcanal.

With the first batch of A6M3s, designated Model 32, there were two points of immediate difference from the Model 11 and Model 21. Of minor though useful importance was the fact that the ammunition supply for the cannon was increased from sixty to 100 rounds per gun. The real point of difference was the fact that for the new aircraft Mitsubishi adopted the 1130hp Sakae 21 engine, complete with two-speed supercharger, in the place of the old but reliable one-speed unit of the Sakae 12. The change had certain unforeseen side effects. Firstly, there were very few Sakae 21 engines available at the time when the development and production of the Model 32 began to get under way. This meant that in the vital numbers game the Japanese lost still more ground to their enemies, having to replace losses rather than increasing and consolidating existing strength. Secondly, the anticipated increase in performance as a result of fitting the Zero with a new, more powerful engine simply did not materialize. It proved capable of making 341mph at 20,000ft and it had a faster rate of climb than the A6M2. The Model 32 did not handle as well as the Model 11 and Model 12 and her overall agility was slightly inferior to that of the earlier models.

In an effort to overcome these problems – and to meet the shrill chorus of protest that came from the operational groups regarding the new aircraft – Mitsubishi removed 1m from the wing span. The tips of the wings were clipped and squared, eliminating the need for folding wing tips to meet elevator dimensions. This had the effect of marginally speeding up production. But the move decreased the wing area by about one square yard, and this did nothing to improve the aircraft's agility. In turning circle and speed of turn the A6M3 was a split second slower than the A6M2, but there were certain compensations. The square-tipped Zero was a fraction faster than the original A6M3, and her diving speed and ability to roll at high speed were both enhanced.

Taken altogether the gains and losses in handling characteristics probably cancelled one another out, which in effect meant that the A6M3 was no advance over the A6M2. In one vital respect the Model 32 was decidedly inferior to the A6M2. The larger engine and supercharger intake necessitated the shifting of the firewall some 8in aft, thereby drastically reducing the amount of fuel carried internally by the aircraft. To compound this problem the new engine was not as economical in its rate of consumption as the less powerful Sakae 12. These two factors had the effect of reducing the range of the Model 32 by 24 percent compared to the Model 21. This was to have unforeseen repercussions in the battles for the Solomons. Pressed into service in a desperate attempt to hold the upper and central Solomons, the A6M3 was forced to operate from bases as far away as 650 miles from Guadalcanal. This gave the Zeros a mere hour at cruising speeds over the island, and this presented considerable, indeed often fatal, problems for Japanese pilots. The fickleness of the weather, with massed cloud banks and violent storms, the problems of accurate navigation and sheer pilot fatigue accounted for many Model 32s which were forced to ditch as their fuel tanks ran dry. Such losses became prohibitive, coming on top of heavy combat losses as a result of the Japanese fighters confronting better pilots in machines only slightly inferior to the Zero. One of the major reasons why the Japanese chose to abandon the struggle for Guadalcanal was the high rate of loss among fighter aircraft, plus the desire to fight the next round of the battle on shorter lines of communications and where the Zero would not be called upon to fight at its extreme range.

The losses suffered by the Model 32 in the course of the Guadalcanal campaign led to the development of the Model 22, which differed from the Model 32 in just one respect. To overcome the problems of insufficient range, 45-liter (9.9-Imp gallon) fuel tanks were located in the wings outboard of the cannon. These tanks restored the range of the Model 22 to that of the A6M2, but without these tanks being self-sealing the vulnerability of the aircraft was simply increased. Overall, Models 32 and 22 proved to be no better and in many ways definitely inferior to Models 11 and 21. What had been conceived as a qualitative improvement over a tried aircraft turned out to be nothing more than an inadequate stopgap. Neither Model of the A6M3 in any way came near to answering the problems facing Japanese fighters. Fitting long-barrelled 20mm cannon to Model 22 and calling it Model 22a was not a solution. By the time the battle for Guadalcanal had been fought and lost, what was desperately needed was a new concept that embraced the Zero's range and agility with greater strength, protection and firepower. In fact such an aircraft was beginning to appear for the first time, but it happened to be an American, not a Japanese, aircraft. Much more time was to be lost and three more variants of the Zero were to give battle at ever-lengthening odds before the Japanese finally produced in late 1944 the fighter that they needed in 1942. That fighter, too, was a Zero variant.

THE A6M5

By the end of the campaign on, around and above Guadalcanal the Japanese were no closer to possessing a suitable replacement for the A6M2 than they had been before the appearance of the A6M3. Despite the high hopes that had been held for it, the Model 32 showed that at high and medium altitudes it was no match for the Lightning and Corsair. It was obvious as 1943 progressed and the new F6F Hellcat appeared on the scene for the first time that the Japanese had to work on something very special if they were to have any reasonable chance of regaining supremacy in the air. In this situation, however, the Japanese were caught by the success of their original Zeros. Because of the seemingly endless problems that beset the J2M and lack of progress being made with the A7M, the Japanese were forced to resort to making modifications of a proven failure – the A6M3 Model 32 – in an effort to counter the growing numerical and qualitative superiority enjoyed by the enemy.

What was absurd was that the qualitative improvement sought in the A6M4 had to be abandoned. This aircraft was conceived as a stopgap until the J2M became available, but because the A6M4 program itself had to be abandoned with just two prototypes built, the Japanese were reduced to adopting another modification of the Model 32. This aircraft, designated the A6M5 Model 52, was superior to the Model 32 but was inferior to the discontinued A6M4. The A6M5 Model 52 in its turn was seen as an interim measure until the A7M appeared. Because the A7M was never produced in sufficient numbers, an aircraft that began life as a substitute for an aircraft that was originally a makeweight finished up in production right up until the end of the war. This aircraft, and its various derivatives, remained Japan's first-line fighter aircraft until August 1945. In any other circumstances such a record of adaptability and flexibility might have been admirable; for Japan in the years 1943 until 1945 this situation was unutterably disastrous.

The story of the A6M5 began and ended in failure, and throughout its period of service it tasted only successive and decisive defeats. The failure in which it was conceived lay in the shortcomings of the A6M2 and A6M3 as revealed in the Solomons and the inability of Japanese industry to overcome the problems that surrounded the development of the A6M4. To achieve a definite qualitative improvement with the A6M4 it was proposed to give the new aircraft a powerpack in the form of a supercharged Sakae engine, but the technical difficulties encountered with this engine proved beyond solution and plans for the production of the aircraft had to be abandoned. This decision, as unavoidable as it was disastrous in its implications, forced the Imperial Navy to turn its attention to seeking improvements and modifications to the Model 32. The new aircraft that was developed as a result was the A6M5 Model 52 which incorporated certain of the later Model 32s in-production improvements as well as other new

Below: **The A6M5 Model 52.**

modifications. Furthermore, the Model 52 was developed at roughly the same time as various other production variations were being developed. In fact three more or less simultaneous variants of the A6M5 were to be developed – the Model 52, the Model 52a and the Model 52b – before the Model 52c entered service after a series of crushing, disastrous defeats in mid-1944. Subsequently it was from the Model 52c that the Japanese sought further developments in the form of the A6M6 Model 53c, the A6M7 Model 63 and, indirectly, the A6M8 Model 64.

Above: **One of the most famous Zeros of the war, a captured A6M5 Type 0 Carrier Fighter Model 52 in the service of the Americans.**

As mentioned earlier, the original Model 52 was a slight improvement over the A6M3 Model 32s, which had been subjected to in-production modifications. The latter-day Model 32s had been improved with new wings with a thicker gauge skin, the most notable feature of the wings being that they were rounded and nonfolding. These basic characteristics were design features and purpose-built in the A6M5 Model 52. The new design permitted the abandonment of folding wings *in toto* and all the mechanisms affecting the folding wings were stripped out. In this the new aircraft differed from the Model 32s which had retained the wing mechanisms even though the wing configurations had been changed. In addition, the ailerons of the Model 52 were faired directly into the rounded wing tips, but in no other respect were the wings any improvement over those of the Model 32. The slight reduction of wing area did not adversely affect maneuverability. This remained high, but like the Model 32 she could not compete at altitude with the Lightnings and Corsairs. She was slightly more maneuverable than the Hellcat but in every other respect she was inferior. She was fatally weak in that the wings carried the same vulnerable fuel tanks in their outboard parts as the Model 32. She carried no extra guns in the wings.

Above: **A Mitsubishi A6M5 Navy Type 0 Fighter Model 52 which was rushed into service in autumn 1943.**

The wing improvements were limited, but, as is so often the case with Japanese equipment and resources during World War II, the improvements did not go far enough. The wings themselves are perfect illustration of this. Because of the extra wing strength the Model 52 was capable of a much faster dive than had been achieved by any previous Zero. At 356 knots (410mph/660kph), the Model 52 was far superior to any earlier A6M, but still could not match the performances of American fighters. And, moreover, speed was not an effective substitute for armor. The defensive weaknesses of the Zero remained unredeemed in the Model 52.

In designing the Model 52, Mitsubishi played safe by keeping to the tried and proven Sakae 21 engine, but overall speed was boosted by the provision of new exhausts being fitted to give some extra power to the aircraft. As a result, despite being nearly 7.5 percent heavier in a loaded state than the A6M3 Model 32, the Model 52 was appreciably faster than previous Zeros. The A6M5 Model 52 was the first Zero to have a maximum speed of over 350mph. She could make 351mph (305 knots or 565kph) at nearly 20,000ft and had a higher service ceiling and rate of climb than the Model 32. But these advantages were gained at a cost of decreased range. The endurance of the Model 52 was inferior to the previous Zeros, but, at the same time, it remained greater than that of any American fighter, Hellcat included. Indeed, until the end of the conflict, the Zero's superior range continued to be one of the very few advantages she retained over American fighters.

The Model 52 went for her service trials in August 1943 and into production in the early months of 1944. This made her almost exactly contemporaneous with the Model 52a. This variant, the A6M5a, differed in two ways from the Model 52. Firstly, the two wing-mounted 20mm Type 99 Mk 3 cannon, which had been in service for some time, were replaced by the Mark 4. This was of some small value because in the place of the 100 rounds a gun carried in drums, the new cannon were belt-fed and supplied with 125 rounds each. Secondly, the skins of the wings were even thicker than ever before, and this made the Model 52a better in a dive than even the Model 52. The Model 52a was much faster in the dive, being able to touch speeds of up to 460mph (399 knots or 741kph). This represented a 13 percent increase in performance over the Model 52 and with this the Mitsubishi design teams were content. They were satisfied that the Zero had reached its optimum diving speed and, indeed, no other Zero, not even those designed and produced later in the war as dive bombers, ever matched this speed. The enhanced diving speed of the Model 52a came as an unpleasant shock to American pilots, but even this increase was not quite enough for the Zero to catch even the Corsair. The latter remained 20mph faster in the dive than the A6M5a, and this took no account of the ever-widening skill differential between American and Japanese pilots at this time.

Slightly behind the Model 52 and the Model 52a in time came the Model 52b. It was with this aircraft that the Japanese belatedly and hesitantly began to move in the direction in which they should have been headed as early as 1942, if not before. The Models 52 and 52a were in the final analysis merely variations on a theme. The theme was basically the speed-maneuver formula, which had been satisfactory in its time, but by 1943/44 was hacknied and discredited. Something extra – namely armor – was needed. With the Model 52b the Japanese took steps, however inadequate, for the first time to work in protection and increased firepower as Kofukuda and Kono

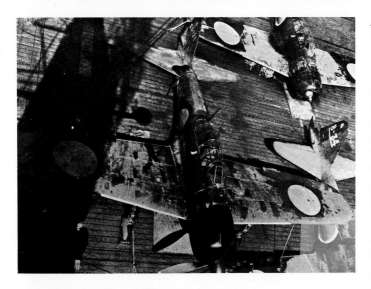

Above: **An A6M5 with surrender markings, a green cross on white background, toward the end of the war.**
Left: **A Model 52 of the Navy Air Corps No 261, probably an A6M5b.**
Left below: **An A6M5c with the extra pair of wing-mounted cannons clearly visible.**

had insisted in 1942. The Model 52b lost one of its 7.7mm machine guns, receiving in its place one 13.2mm (0.52in) cannon. This gun and the remaining 7.7mm machine gun were fuselage-mounted. With this armament the A6M5b Model 52b was unique among Zeros in that it carried weapons of three different calibers. Equally novel was the incorporation of a protected windshield. This consisted of two spaced layers of plastic between glass, the thickness of the whole being about 2in (51mm). One might criticize this on the grounds that it was totally inadequate, but it was better than nothing, and that was what Japanese pilots had had before the Model 52b. In addition the fuel tanks were fitted for the first time with fire extinguishers, filled with carbon dioxide, in an effort to eliminate one of the glaring weaknesses of the Zero.

The Model 52b represented the best of the Zeros to see combat. It was far superior to anything that had gone before and anything that came after, but was delivered in too few numbers to be effective. Time was running out for Japan, and later versions of the Zero were produced in insufficient numbers to make anything but the slightest imprint on a by-then overwhelming American preponderance of strength. As it was in the early months of 1944, Japanese factories strained every muscle in order that as many Model 52, 52a and 52bs could be produced as quickly as possible. The Imperial Navy had good reason to urge construction: it knew that in the course of 1944 it had to concentrate as many aircraft as possible in order to face the most critical encounters Japan had to fight in the Pacific War.

2

43-188

1

1. A Mitsubishi A6M5, typical of the aircraft that were in service from carriers and shore bases in the spring of 1944.
2. An A6M5a which was found on Guam Island in 1944. It was returned to Japan and carefully restored and is now kept as a training model.
3. A Zero Model 52 fighter undergoing restoration in California. It was found at Aslite airport on Saipan.

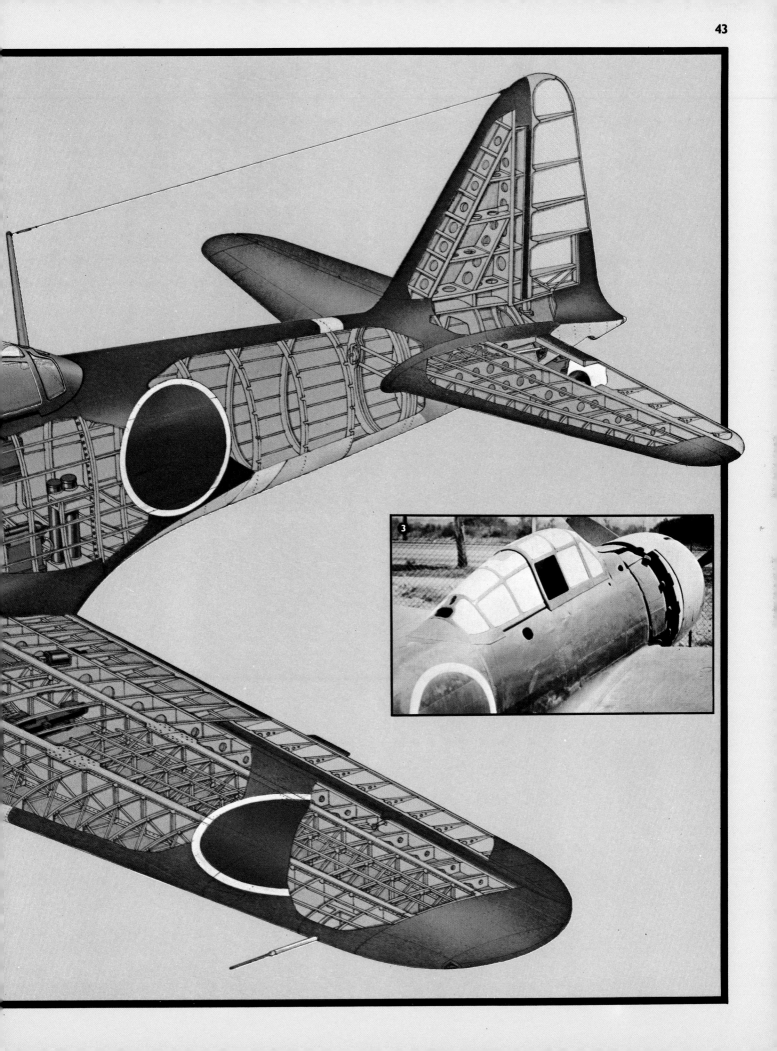

3

44

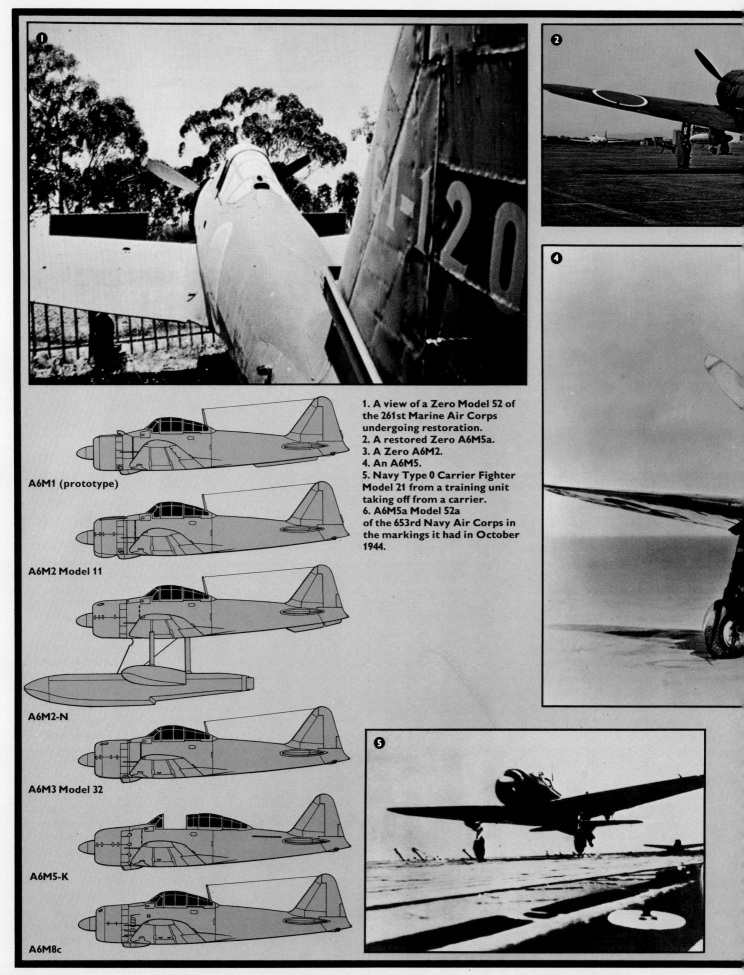

A6M1 (prototype)

A6M2 Model 11

A6M2-N

A6M3 Model 32

A6M5-K

A6M8c

1. A view of a Zero Model 52 of the 261st Marine Air Corps undergoing restoration.
2. A restored Zero A6M5a.
3. A Zero A6M2.
4. An A6M5.
5. Navy Type 0 Carrier Fighter Model 21 from a training unit taking off from a carrier.
6. A6M5a Model 52a of the 653rd Navy Air Corps in the markings it had in October 1944.

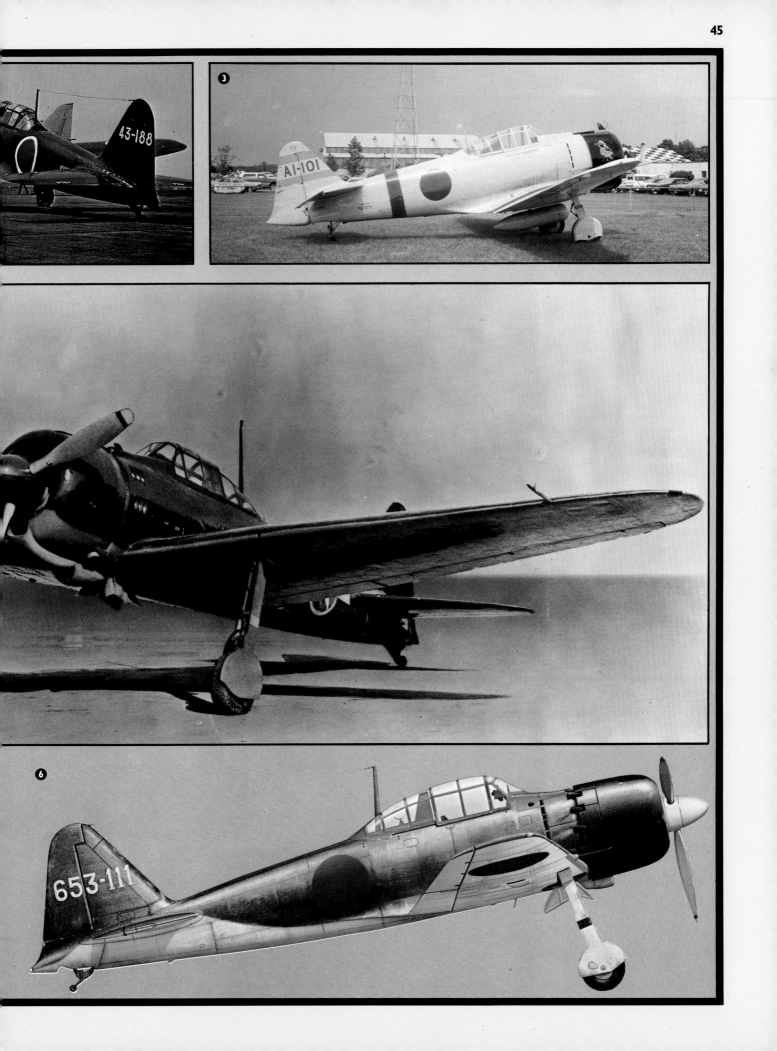

3

43-188

AI-101

6

653-111

THE CRISIS OF THE EM

With the defeat of the Japanese in the Solomons, the Americans had started on a step-by-step reduction of the Bismarcks. By the beginning of 1944 the Japanese position in these islands was in ruins and Allied forces in the Southwest Pacific stood on the brink of a series of moves that, with alarming rapidity, was to wrench the position of the Japanese in the island chains of Southeast Asia wide open. At the same time, however, in November 1943 the Americans began their increasingly dynamic drive across the central Pacific, starting with a landing on the atoll of Tarawa in the Gilberts. Strategically the Japanese were caught in a terrible dilemma that grew more agonizing with every passing week. Trying to hold a central position between two thrusts, neither of which was necessarily inferior to the force Japan had available, did not deter an attack nor offer an effective defense of Japanese conquests. In the long term the attempt to hold a position between the developing threats could end only in total defeat and disaster. Yet given Japanese inferiority in the air, the once all-conquering Navy could not hope to challenge either of these developing threats.

In the course of 1943 and early 1944 the Imperial Navy was caught in a strategic position riddled with glaring inconsistencies. It had to conserve and expand its strength, particularly in the air. This could only be achieved by declining battle, which was politically and strategically impossible. Japan had to force rather than decline battle. The Japanese were aware that by waiting, the balance of power tilted ever more against them because of the superior resources of the USA. To risk an action against the rampaging American carriers without a total concentration of air resources was to invite defeat. At the same time Japan had to try to counter any American breach of her perimeter defenses and she had to commit her forces to wear down the Americans to the point where the Imperial Navy might risk action with some reasonable hope of success. If Japan were to attempt this, however, she had to commit those very forces she was trying to husband and preserve for 'the decisive battle,' knowing full well that those forces were highly unlikely to inflict disproportionately heavy losses on the Americans. Japan was working on a declining scale of power, and the situation in which she found herself was an impossible one.

In the face of these mounting threats to their position in the western Pacific, the Japanese carried out the only policy possible. Although they recognized that in 1944 full-scale naval battle had been avoided since the Midway defeat, with just one exception, it would have to be faced. The Japanese, moreover, recognized that the outcome of this battle would decide the war. This battle had to be given as the Americans moved into the western Pacific toward the Philippines. For Japan the Philippines had to be her *ne plus ultra* line because the breaching of the barrier presented by the islands would result inevitably in the severing of Japan's lines of communications with Malaya and the Indies. From these two areas Japan drew a whole host of raw materials, especially oil, on which Japanese industry was dependent. If the Japanese lines of communication with Malaya and the Indies were cut, then the Japanese cause would be beyond recall. Thus in order to give battle before the Philippines the Japanese deployed major land-based forces in support of their carefully preserved carrier forces. Accordingly the A6M5s were concentrated, mainly with the carriers, to give battle in the Philippine Sea in June 1944 following the American invasion of the Marianas. The gravity of the situation for Japan can be gauged by the fact that for this battle the assembled carrier forces constituted the most powerful single force ever assembled by the Imperial Navy in the course of the Pacific War.

For the battle of the Philippine Sea the Imperial Navy assembled a force of five battleships, thirteen cruisers and 28 destroyers in support of nine carriers. On the carriers were deployed 450 aircraft of which exactly half were Zeros, nearly all of them A6M5s. The distribution of aircraft among the carriers was as follows:

	A6M	B6N (Jill)*	B5N (Kate)*	D3A (Val)**	D4Y/22 (Judy)**
1st Carrier Division: CVA *Shokaku*, CVA *Taiho*, CVA *Zuikaku*	81	54	0	0	90***
2nd Carrier Divisions: CVA *Hiyo*, CVA *Junyo*, CVL *Ryuho*	81	27	0	27	9
3rd Carrier Division: CVL *Chitose*, CVL *Chiyoda*, CVL *Zuiho*	63	6	12	0	0

* Torpedo bombers or bombers.
** Dive bombers.
***Including nine D4Y Model 11s for reconnaissance purposes.

Note: CVA is the standard signature for fleet carriers. CVL is the standard signature for light carriers. Escort carriers are designated CVE.

Right: **A Japanese bomber out of control during the Battle of the Philippine Sea.**
Below: **US carrier aircraft hit Ushi airfield on Tinian in June 1944.**

Above: **The scene on board the USS** *Monterey* **at the height of the Philippine Sea battle in June 1944. An F6F Hellcat is catapulted off to undertake a defensive patrolling mission.**

In support of the carriers were some 550 land-based aircraft spread in a vast arc between New Guinea and the Marianas. The Japanese planned to use the superior range of their aircraft to discover the whereabouts of the American carriers and to hit the Americans as soon as they approached. The Japanese intended to use the superior range of their attack aircraft to strike at the Americans while their carriers remained outside the range of any American counterstrike. In order to use their carrier aircraft to maximum effect the Japanese intended to stage them through their island airfields.

The weaknesses of the Japanese plan were numerous. The American 5th Fleet possessed fifteen attack carriers in its Task Forces. These carried 891 aircraft, and in support were eleven escort carriers and 879 land-based aircraft, from the three American services (Army, Navy and Marine Corps). In addition, the Americans held the initiative, and could choose the time and place for their attack, possibly being able to concentrate on overwhelming one part of the Japanese forces before the others could come to its aid. The Japanese were being forced to react to the moves of a superior enemy across thousands of miles of sea and sky. In this situation speed of concentration and local superiority of numbers, almost by definition, were denied the Japanese. At the very best the decision to give battle in the Philippine Sea represented a desperate gamble for the Japanese.

From disastrous start to catastrophic finish the Battle of the Philippine Sea was for the Japanese a tale of woe, mitigated only by continuous claims by the Japanese of glowing success and massive damage that owed more to the imagination than reality. But a brief account of the battle is in order to illustrate the performance of the Zero and the use, or misuse, of naval aviation by the Japanese in the course of the battle.

The engagement was marked on the Japanese side by aggression and mismanagement. The Americans, on the other hand, after having cut loose across the central Pacific with a series of savage attacks, fought for the most part a cool, cautious and calculated battle. Unaware of the whereabouts of the Japanese carriers, the Americans stood off eastward as far as possible, firstly annihilating Japanese land-based airpower in the Marianas. Until Japanese airpower in these islands was broken the Americans had no intention of making any major

movement to the west. In defense of the Marianas the Japanese, caught with divided forces that were unable to support one another, squandered their precious resources in giving battle against impossible odds. They lost over half of their available land-based aircraft without inflicting any appreciable loss on the Americans in return. Incredibly, the carrier force was not informed of this defeat or of the fact that negligible support from land-based forces could be expected for the forthcoming battle.

After having discovered the American fleet with its long-range reconnaissance aircraft, the Japanese carriers launched the first of their attacks early on 19 June 1944. Beyond American range these attacks were made by massed but ever dwindling formations. The Americans refused to be drawn into seeking offensive action against the Japanese carriers with their strike aircraft. Instead, the Americans chose to rely on massive defensive patrolling by Hellcats to keep the attacking Japanese at arm's length. If battle was joined over the carriers then the Americans were dependent on the massed firepower from battleships, cruisers and destroyers to protect the all-important aircraft carriers. By these tactics the Americans destroyed the carriers as effectively as if they had sunk them, the value of a carrier being dependent only on the strength and effectiveness of its aircraft. In every attack the Japanese bombers were given totally inadequate numerical protection by the Zeros. In their attacks the fighter element numbered about one-third of all aircraft: in order to have any chance of success the Japanese needed to have at least doubled the number of fighters provided as escorts. The weakness of the number of escorts put into the air by the Japanese was accentuated by the inferiority of Japanese pilots and aircraft compared to their American counterparts. Despite flying in a new formation of three flights of four, breaking into pairs with the more experienced pilot leading when contact with the enemy was obtained, the Zeros proved totally incapable of defending themselves, still less the heavily loaded and vulnerable bombers.

The American tactics of letting the Japanese come to them resulted in the systematic massacre of successive waves of attacking aircraft, and by the end of the Japanese effort on the 20th only twenty bombers (of all types) and 25 Zero fighters remained with the carriers. The remainder had been either destroyed by American fighters or brought down by gunfire. To make matters worse for the Japanese two of their fleet carriers had succumbed to submarine attack. The cost to the Americans was precisely 26 combat losses among their aircraft and minimal damage to their ships. American air losses were increased by accidents and by the deliberate commitment of strike aircraft late on the 20th when, after two days of battle, the Japanese carrier force was finally located by American reconnaissance aircraft. The Japanese carriers, unaware of the extent of their own losses and misled into believing that grave losses had been inflicted on the Americans, made the mistake of lingering too long in the danger zone. A total of 216 American aircraft were committed to the attack, the inherent risks of a night recovery being accepted. Nearly half the American aircraft committed to the attack were lost, though many of the air crew were later recovered. But in return the American aircraft, brushing aside the feeble resistance put up by the Japanese carrier aircraft, sank the *Hiyo* and extensively damaged two of the surviving fleet carriers, a battleship and a cruiser. The Japanese, breaking off action at best possible speed, steered for Okinawa, knowing that the decisive battle of the war had been fought and lost. Never again were the Japanese able to put a balanced carrier force to sea in order to offer battle: the only subsequent use of the carrier force was at Leyte Gulf in October where it was used as a sacrificial bait in an attempt to lure the American carriers away from the scene of invasion, thereby allowing the surface ships of the Imperial Navy to break through to cause havoc among the American forces. This role, played with fatalistic brilliance, was almost successful. The Americans took the bait and bared their invasion forces, but the Japanese surface ships, for reasons that have never been properly explained, failed to capitalize on the situation.

Below: **A damaged Zero which was captured by the Americans at Buna airstrip in New Guinea.**

AFTERMATH OF THE P

To any thinking Japanese who was aware of the true facts of the Philippine Sea, the war was lost. Yet for political reasons to admit this was impossible, and Japan still hoped, if not to retrieve something from the wreckage of her plans of conquest, then at least to avoid the ignominy of unconditional surrender and occupation. Given that Japan still held vast tracts of territory – in China, elsewhere on the Asian mainland and throughout the island chains of Southeast Asia – great powers, if only of destruction, remained to her. It was inconceivable that Japan would accept defeat in 1944. As events were to show, not even two atomic bombs in August 1945 were enough to convince half the ruling military hierarchy that the reality of unconditional surrender had to be faced.

The defeat at the Battle of the Philippine Sea therefore served only to add urgency to the task of procuring new weapons with which to try to stave off defeat, and from the battle there were two major developments concerning the Mitsubishi Zero. The first was of a purely tactical nature. Despite all their shortcomings in the June battle, the Zeros had shown certain previously-unsuspected qualities. The A6M5s, like all their predecessors, had carried a fuselage-mounted drop tank of 330 liters (72.9 Imp gallons), but in preparing for the Philippine Sea some 63 Zeros, those of the 3rd Carrier Division, had been modified to carry a single 250kg (551lb) bomb and had been pressed into service as dive bombers. Such aircraft had been concentrated with the light carriers because the new D4Y Suisei (Allied codename 'Judy') dive bomber proved unable to operate off the restricted lengths of the smaller carriers. With this massive load the Zero was drastically encumbered to the serious detriment of speed and maneuverability, but that the Zero could lift such a bomb load at all was remarkable. Its accuracy in dive-bombing attacks, though not good, was not inferior to purpose-built aircraft. Assuming the ever-declining quality of Japanese pilots, the obvious weaknesses of the Zero and the effective writing-off of the carriers as a fighting force, there remained the ingredients for a radical departure from conventional naval aviation practice.

This departure, of course, was the move in favor of kamikaze attacks. With hopelessly outclassed aircraft and pilots who could not be expected to survive a combat mission against F6Fs, the deliberate use of obsolete aircraft and barely trained pilots for suicide attacks made common sense. The Japanese still possessed many aircraft, none of which were effective in conventional terms, and there was no shortage of volunteers among the air crews for one-way missions in the service of the Emperor. Initially the old A6M2s were considered the most easily expendable of Japan's vulnerable aircraft, but ultimately virtually every type of aircraft was pressed into service and nearly all production of conventional aircraft was to be ended in favor of kamikaze production.

The kamikazes (the word means 'Divine Wind' after the storms that wrecked the fleets of Kublai Khan in 1281 and thus saved Japan from an invasion she could not resist) eventually worked out comprehensive tactics in order to inflict the greatest possible damage on the enemy. Naturally, much of the evolution of tactics had to be theoretical because there was no debriefing after missions. The most favored tactics involved an approach to contact at low altitude under the protection of the most modern aircraft, flown by the most experienced pilots of a formation. Ideally, the escorts drew fire from the massed banks of secondary and tertiary armaments of the escort ships while the kamikazes made their attacks. It was best if such attacks could be synchronized with conventional attacks that would hold the attention of the American combat air patrols. The most favored advance to contact for suicide pilots was from astern of the carriers where anti-aircraft fire might be expected to be at its minimum. From this approach the kamikazes had the options of attempting to smash into the poorly protected hulls of American ships or, preferably, to climb rapidly in the last one or two minutes of flight (thus giving the CAP as little time to react as possible) before plunging down on the target at a very steep angle. Invariably it was the American fleet carriers that were the ideal target for such attacks, their forward elevators being singled out for special attention. Wrecking this part of the ship offered the Japanese their best chance of either totally incapacitating or destroying a carrier.

The systematic use of kamikaze tactics – there had been impromptu performances earlier in the war by pilots of stricken aircraft – began on 21 October 1944 after the American landings on Leyte in the Philippines. The first two missions had to be abandoned because the American forces could not be located, but the third, on 25 October, resulted in an American escort group being very badly mauled. The small American carriers were taken by surprise by the deliberate

Right: **The carrier** *Belleau Wood* **comes under attack at the height of the Battle of Leyte Gulf, October 1944.**
Below: **A Judy bomber is destroyed as it attempts to crash into the** *Wasp* **off the Ryukyus in March 1945.**

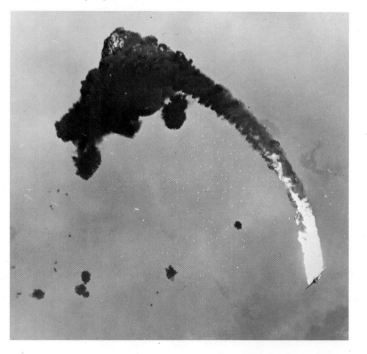

HILIPPINE SEA

1. Six members of the newly formed Kamikaze Corps, which was founded by Rear Admiral Onishi in a last bid to stave off defeat.
2. A kamikaze pilot on Kyushu before his final flight to Okinawa.
3. Kamikaze pilots ready for their final mission.
4. A Zero kamikaze plane takes off from a Philippine airport in October 1944.
5. Fire-control parties deal with two kamikaze planes on the USS *Saratoga* during bombardment operations on Iwo Jima.

use of A6M2s (escorted by A6M5s) in the suicide role. In this attack the Japanese accounted for the *St Lo* (CVE 63) which was quite literally blown to pieces by a kamikaze that penetrated deep inside her. Three other escort carriers were heavily damaged, one of which, the *Suwannee*, was singled out for further severe punishment the following day.

The attack of 25 October established what for Allied seamen was to become an all too familiar pattern for the next nine months. The main effort of the kamikaze attacks was to be expended in the futile defense of the Philippines, Okinawa and Iwo Jima. The last-ditch defense of the Japanese homeland by various types of suicide weapons was averted by the precipitous surrender of the Imperial Government in August 1945. In the Philippines nearly eighty percent of all suicide aircraft were Zero-sens, mostly A6M2s, and it would seem unlikely that the proportion of Zeros among the kamikazes was much lower in either of the two subsequent campaigns.

In reality the kamikazes achieved very little. They were at best a wasting asset, their effectiveness always decreasing as their surprise value disappeared, the standard of pilot training plumbed new lows and the Americans thickened up their air patrols. Moreover, the Japanese pilots could not always show selectivity in their choice of targets, and their various attacks could not be co-ordinated in order to split fire or tie down American fighter aircraft. There was a natural tendency to attack the first enemy ships located rather than search for the heavily protected carriers, and as a result much of the kami-

kaze effort was expended against the destroyers forming the radar picket line. Apart from the *St Lo*, no ship larger than a destroyer was ever sunk by suicide aircraft, though several cruisers almost spoiled this record. Many ships suffered various degrees of damage. Off Okinawa, for example, suicide aircraft sank 25 Allied ships and damaged a further 157. Nearly 100 other ships were damaged as a result of near misses. Yet given the heavy concentrations of shipping off Okinawa such losses were light – though not in human terms – and successes against the heavy American carriers were few and far between. The Japanese would have been far better advised to have mounted a sustained submarine offensive against the carriers' oilers and the carriers as they moved eastward for replenishment than to have persisted in suicide attacks. It is not without interest to note that two of Japan's better results against American carriers (the *Princeton* which was sunk, and the *Franklin* which was ripped apart by explosions but somehow managed to survive) were registered by conventional aircraft. The use of suicide tactics was an admittance of bankruptcy on the part of the Imperial Navy and its air arm, and no number of A6M2s or any other make or mark of aircraft assigned a suicide role could alter the fact that there was no effective substitute for orthodox air power.

Below: Gone were the days when the Zero and its pilot were at least the equal of its opponents. In this series of action shots a Zero is easily shot down.

PHOTO SECTION
5TH FIGHTER COMMAND   1 0 SEP 1943

Above: **These A6M5c Zeros and A6M5-K two-seater trainers stationed in Korea were Japan's last line of defense.**
Left: **Captured Zeros are ferried back to the USA after the war.**

The extent to which Japan's conventional air power had declined both in aircraft and pilot quality is evident in just two engagements that took place in 1944 as the Americans closed in on Japan. On 24 June eighty of the newest A6M5s, split into high and low formations, caught an inferior number of Hellcats over Iwo Jima opening up their formation as they climbed through cloud into clear sky. As the Americans emerged they were bounced immediately by the high formation, coming at the inferior and for the moment slower Hellcats. Scattering, the F6Fs had to dive into the Japanese low formation which was concentrated and ready. As the Americans came into the low formation the engagement became a free-for-all. The Japanese shot down twelve Hellcats. Most of these fell to a very few experienced pilots in the high group: most of the Japanese pilots failed to make anything of their fleeting opportunity to catch the superior American aircraft at a disad-

vantage. In return the Hellcats, despite being taken by surprise and at a considerable tactical disadvantage, accounted for no less than forty Zeros. On 24 October a total force of seven Hellcats encountered a Japanese force of thirty Zeros and thirty bombers off the Philippines moving out to attack American carriers. Five Hellcats took on the bombers and accounted for nine of them. The two remaining Hellcats tackled the Zeros and shot down no less than fourteen of them. In desperation the Japanese Zeros had to form a circle in an attempt to hold off the Americans, but even this did not work. No American aircraft were lost in this action. Neither Japan's aircraft nor her pilots could match those of the United States, and in the whole of the Philippines campaign it has been estimated that the Japanese suffered about 4000 combat losses, of which about 650 were suicide aircraft. (The Americans, in contrast, lost about 800 aircraft from all causes.) Japanese losses were doubled as a result of landing accidents and various other unknown causes, and it has been estimated that at least half of all Japanese air losses in World War II were sustained outside of combat and were the result of pilot error, mechanical failure or weather or other nonmilitary cause.

The second development that arose from the Philippine Sea disaster was the Imperial Navy's placing of yet another order for yet another improved version of the Zero. The order was given out on 23 July – a tacit admittance of defeat in the battle of the Philippine Sea and the critical nature of Japan's position. The result was the development of the A6M5c Model 52c, of which only 93 were ever built. For the very first time the specifications drawn up by the Imperial Navy for this aircraft included protection for the pilot on the scale that he deserved. This was to be provided in the form of an armored windshield and a toughened-steel plate under the pilot's seat, behind which was to be located a self-sealing tank containing 31 gallons (140 liters) of fuel. This belated attention to protection was stressed, as was offensive power. The sole surviving 7.7mm gun was suppressed, but two 13.2mm cannon were mounted outboard of the undercarriage.

Mitsubishi believed it could meet these demands of the Navy with ease, but the whole of order was thrown into complete confusion by a series of seemingly irresponsible decisions. To meet the Imperial Navy's demand that the new aircraft should show no falling off of overall Zero performance, Mitsubishi correctly calculated that the A6M5c would have to be at least 600lb heavier than the A6M5b. Such a weight increase was inevitable in order to carry the armor, to strengthen the wings to take the extra guns and racks for air-to-air missiles and to take the stress of 460mph dives. But if the aircraft was to retain its speed and agility, then it was obviously underpowered if the Sakae 21 engine was retained. The chief designer of Mitsubishi, Eitaro Sano, more or less demanded that Mitsubishi's own Kinsei (Golden Star) 62 engine should be used in the A6M5c. Sano reasoned that as the Kinsei was nearly 250hp greater than the Sakae 21, it was the only engine that could allow the A6M5c to compete on anything like equal terms with the Hellcat. Mitsubishi's arguments were rejected by the Navy. Under the prompting of

Below: **A6M5c Zeros stationed in Korea are prepared for takeoff.**

Nakajima, the Navy argued that if the Sakae 21 engine was modified to include a water-methanol injection system, then the Model 52c would be sufficiently high-powered in short-duration bursts for combat with the Hellcat. Speed of construction was all-important to the Navy. The development of the Kinsei did not promise extra power but threatened extra delay. After the fiasco of the Philippine Sea and the certainty that the Philippines themselves were to be attacked shortly, the Imperial Navy needed aircraft desperately and was prepared to take short cuts. The problem for Mitsubishi was that the modified Sakae engine (the 31A) was not fully tested and ready for installation. In any event the Navy drastically overrated the performance that might have been expected from such an engine. Consequently the Model 52c was supplied with the Sakae 21 and was drastically underpowered as a result. There was nothing that the Navy and Mitsubishi could do about this situation.

Nevertheless, what is remarkable about the A6M5c is the fact that the first production-model was ready in early September, less than two months after it was ordered and more than a month before the invasion of the Philippines. By prodigies of effort and improvisation a joint Navy-Mitsubishi team actually managed to build a production-model in not much more than six weeks. By any standard this was a remarkable achievement, but it was one that turned sour on the team that had worked so hard to produce the machine. The Model 52c, despite having had its wings strengthened, was not up to the demands placed on it and had to have the wings strengthened still further in order to give the aircraft greater rigidity. The Sakae 21 engine had to be used because the Sakae 31A was not available, and the performance of the Model 52a fell away very badly. Perhaps most frustrating of all, when production started, the ordered self-sealing fuel tanks were not available. Very few had been produced and neither the production nor ground crews knew how to fit them. Therefore the Model 52c as produced had neither the power nor the vital tanks that were essential. To add insult to injury once the first Model 52c aircraft began to come off the production lines both the promised engines and the protected tanks became

available, not that that could have been much comfort to the pilots of the A6M5c, the most vulnerable of all the Zeros.

Of the many accusations that can be levelled against the Imperial Navy and Mitsubishi, lack of persistence was not one of them. Once the Sakae 31A engine and self-sealing tanks became available in November 1944, production of the grossly inadequate Model 52c was halted as the weary design teams redrafted plans to meet the Imperial Navy's July specifications. Thus was conceived the A6M6c Model 53c. Here, finally, the material failed the Mitsubishi design teams. The new engine proved highly erratic and totally unreliable and could not generate the power Nakajima had claimed for it. Its teething and maintenance problems proved major headaches and Mitsubishi produced just one version before giving up in despair. Nakajima, perhaps feeling a greater responsibility for the disastrous state of affairs, persisted in production at its

Below: **A captured A6M5 in flight.**

Koizuma plant until early 1945 when it, too, halted production. The end was almost in sight for the Imperial Navy, Mitsubishi, Nakajima and for Japan herself.

One can never be sure whether or not the Japanese were merely deluding themselves, but in the middle of technical failures, natural disaster in the form of an earthquake, devastation caused by mounting bombing raids, and the increasing shortage of manpower and raw materials, the ever-resourceful Mitsubishi managed to produce two more versions of the Zero before the end of the war. That even in her death rattle Japan could still do this, and put into the air for the first time new aircraft that were the best Zeros built to date, does command admiration. In fact the last version of the Zero ever produced by Mitsubishi was a very good aircraft; for Japan the pity of it was that it was three years too late.

The first of the two variants was the A6M7 Model 63. This

Above: **An A6M5 captured on Peleliu in the Central Pacific Area.**
Left: **Japanese cities, particularly Tokyo, were not properly defended against American bombing raids in 1945.**

was the first Zero purpose-built as a dive bomber. It could trace its ancestry back to those Zeros that had been with the 3rd Carrier Division in June 1944, but it differed from the earlier Zero dive bombers in that the early ones were improvised aircraft. The A6M7 had its tailpiece especially strengthened to withstand the effects of a power dive, the whole aircraft gaining strength and rigidity as a result of the change. But the most obvious point of difference from earlier versions was that the A6M7 was installed with a proper bomb rack and release mechanism. These allowed the aircraft to carry either a 250kg or 500kg bomb under the fuselage. This mounting necessitated the removal of the drop tank, but in its place the new aircraft was given two wing-mounted drop tanks, fitted outboard of the cannon. Both tanks were of a 150-liters (33 gallon) capacity. Production of this version of the Zero began in May 1945, but it is unknown how many aircraft were completed. It is known, however, that some of the A6M7s were used as suicide aircraft in the last weeks of the war.

The second of the aircraft to be developed was the A6M8c Model 54c and this aircraft, by common consent, was the best of all the Zeros produced in the war. There is the obvious irony that its high quality was far too late to have any effect on the course of the war, but there was a hidden, bitter irony surrounding the origins of the aircraft. That it appeared at all was the result of Nakajima abandoning the Sakae 31A development program in favor of the more powerful Homare (Honor) engine which it proposed not to use in the Zero but in other, heavier aircraft. Nakajima's ending of production of the Sakae left the way clear for the adoption of the Kinsei 62 as the powerpack for the new Zero. This, of course, was what Sano and Mitsubishi had been wanting all along, but it was not until late November 1944, when the failure of the Sakae 31A became obvious, that the Imperial Navy gave formal approval for the use of the engine. Thus four invaluable months had been allowed to slip by, and there can be no doubt that Nakajima's role in the whole tangled process was pernicious, to say the least. There can be no doubt that, had the Kinsei been given priority over the Sakae in July 1944, the overall result would have been better for Japan. By the division of her resources Japan had produced very few, poor quality aircraft. If she had backed the Kinsei, the final result could hardly have been worse than the one achieved, not that the outcome of the war would have been altered.

The A6M8c Model 54c used the same basic airframe as the A6M7, but the more powerful 1560hp engine was larger than any previous powerpack installed in a Zero. Its extra size necessitated a redesign of the forward fuselage and the elimination of the centrally-mounted 13.2mm cannon. This was a very reasonable price to pay for the reliability and speed the Kinsei conferred on the Zero. The A6M8c also incorporated various improvements that had been slowly gaining acceptance as the fortunes of the Imperial Navy ebbed. All fuel tanks were self-sealing and the fire-extinguishing system was improved considerably. The two wing-mounted drop tanks of the A6M7 were enlarged to carry 350 liters (77 gallons) each. This enabled the new Zero to carry a single 250kg or 500kg bomb to greater ranges than had been possible with earlier aircraft. The A6M8c was equipped to carry eight 10kg (22lb) air-to-air missiles. Certain previous models had been thus equipped, the first being the Model 52b, but by 1945 these were considered a standard feature for attacking the heavy bombers – such as the B-29 Superfortress which was then being used in the bombing of the Japanese homeland. These extra loads the A6M8c could carry at a speed faster than any previous Zero. The Model 54c had a faster rate of climb than any earlier A6M, being able to reach nearly 20,000ft in 6 minutes 50 seconds. At that height she had a maximum speed of 309 knots (356mph or 573kph). Despite being heavier than most Zeros and having a higher weight loading and a lower power loading than any previous Zero, the A6M8c still retained remarkable agility, even though she showed signs of poor workmanship and shoddy finishing. The latter was the inevitable result of the circumstances under which the aircraft was produced. But in her trials she proved surprisingly trouble-free. There were problems of engine-overheating and low oil pressure, but these were quickly and easily resolved.

Not surprisingly the Imperial Navy saw the A6M8c aircraft as the answer to the ubiquitous Hellcat. Accordingly it gave out orders for 6300 of the new Zeros (simply designated the A6M8 Model 64) with instructions for all of Mitsubishi's and Nakajima's factories to start immediate production of the aircraft. Such orders were nonsensical at this stage of the war. With probably less than 18,000 fighters produced by Japan throughout the whole of the Pacific War, to give an order for over 6000 aircraft as an immediate priority was unrealistic. Even if the factories had been able to produce the aircraft there would have been neither the pilots nor the fuel to get them into the air. Yet the A6M8 would have been a remarkable aircraft, and a mere glance at her statistical data, when set against that of the Hellcat, is illuminating:

	The A6M8	The F6F-3
Span	36ft 1.06in	42ft 10in
Length	30ft 3.66in	33ft 7in
Height	11ft 11.22in	13ft 1in
Wing Area	229.27sq ft	334sq ft
Wing Loading	30.3lb/sq ft	36lb/sq ft
Weights: Empty	3,704lb	9,042lb
Loaded	5,313lb	12,186lb
Maximum	6,164lb	13,228lb
Powerpack	1,560hp	2,200hp (later versions)
Maximum Speed	356mph	376mph
Initial rate of climb	2,882ft/minute	3,240ft/minute
Service Ceiling	37,075ft	37,500ft
Range	Unknown	1,090 miles (internal fuel only)
Armament	Two 0.787in and two 0.519in cannon (125rpg) One 1,102lb bomb Up to eight rockets	Six 0.5in machine guns (400rpg) Up to 2,000lb of bombs Up to six rockets

Right: **This Zero fighter crashed on an airstrip in the Korako area, a few miles south of Aitape, New Guinea.**
Bottom: **This Zero Model 52 of the 261st Navy Air Corps was captured in Saipan in June 1944.**
Below: **A6M5 Zero photographed at Omura Base.**

Conflict between the F6F-3 and the A6M8 would have been interesting from the technical point of view, but one surprising fact that emerges from the comparative figures is the imbalance between the weights of the aircraft. The weight of the A6M8 varied between 40.97 percent and 46.60 percent of that of the Hellcat, the overall average being 43.72 percent. It is an open question whether the Japanese were naive in believing that with an aircraft less than half the size of the most formidable carrier aircraft in the world they could regain air supremacy or whether the American achievement in building such a heavy aircraft was an even more outstanding achievement than is recognized generally. In both cases, the Hellcat and the Zero reflected the performance of their respective nations in the course of the Pacific War. The Hellcat represented the massive durability of the great democracy, mobilized for total war. It was tough, hard-hitting and rugged. It was not particularly pleasing to the eye, but added to strength and firepower was numerical strength. In two years between 1943 and 1945 more Hellcats entered service than Zeros were built between 1939 and 1945. The Zero, on the other hand, was mercurial. Elegant and agile, graceful yet brittle, the Zero reflected the lack of strength that plagued Japan in a war which she initiated but in which the Americans rewrote the rules.

Depite the orders of the Imperial Navy not one A6M8 was completed by the time of the final surrender. Completed in April 1945, flown for the first time in May, and hopefully the first of a breed that would wrest command of the air from the Americans, the A6M8c turned out to be the last in the line of famous fighter aircraft. There was to be a certain ironic, bitter 'honor' awaiting the Japanese aviation industry as the war drew to a close and Allied warships began to move into Japanese territorial waters. The factories that had produced the finest fighter aircraft in the world, the fighter that had led an attack that had seen the mightiest and proudest of the European empires humbled and prostrated, were themselves the recipients of the last shells fired from the guns of a British battleship. That the target was Hitachi and not the more deserving Mitsubishi was of no real account. The wheel had come full circle.

Below: **A captured A6M2 with flaps lowered and undercarriage extended.**

APPENDICES

1. The minor Zero variants

The A6M2-K

The Zero naturally presented itself as an ideal aircraft for training purposes, and one of the surprising facts to emerge from the Pacific War is that the two-seater Zero trainer, the A6M2-K, remained in production until the very last month of the war. Though late in starting production, this aircraft effectively outlived any other Zero, including the famous A6M2 itself.

The first prototype trainer was produced in early 1942 and production of the aircraft was given formally in the 1942 17-Shi program. This, of course, was at the time when the A6M2 itself was beginning to show signs of wear and tear and was being phased out slowly by the new A6M3. Rather strangely in view of the general exactness with which the Imperial Navy designated its aircraft, the trainer was designated the A6M2-K Type 0 Trainer-Fighter Model 11. This designation indicated that the aircraft was a modification of the basic A6M2 Model 11, but one would have expected the Japanese to have been exact and to have given the aircraft a quite separate and chronologically correct identity.

The trainer entered production with the Model 21 being used as the basic aircraft, and in every major respect the A6M2-K was similar to the A6M2 Model 21. The trainer, however, was slower, not quite so maneuverable and had a shorter range than the combat version. In appearance it could be distinguished with ease from the first-line Zeros by its enlarged and lengthened cockpit. This was in two parts. The trainee, in the front seat, sat in an open cockpit; the instructor was in an enclosed (and warmer) space. Naturally dual controls were incorporated into the aircraft, but to aid stability and to help recovery in the event of loss of control, small horizontal fins were built into the rear of the fuselage. In order to accommodate the extra person and equipment, the aircraft was lightened by the removal of the heavy undercarriage fittings and the 20mm cannon. Overall the A6M2-K was a most useful aircraft, being conceived and used as the last trainer in the process of working up the trainees from older aircraft to combat versions. Most of the training with the A6M2-K was not done at the Navy's training schools but with operational groups. The general decline in the quality of Japanese pilots that took place in the course of the Pacific War cannot be attributed to any shortcoming of the A6M2-K, but to the general circumstances of the Imperial Navy.

The first A6M2-K production-model was completed in November 1943 by the 21st Naval Air Arsenal at Omura. This ordnance factory had been the producer of the first prototypes and in all built 236 two-seater trainers for the Imperial Navy. The other contractor for the A6M2-K was Hitachi. It was given its first orders in early 1944, and between May 1944 and July 1945 produced 272 trainers. In fact Hitachi was given orders for more than 650 trainers, but the company was unable to set up the production lines quickly enough. It did produce, however, seven A6M5-K two-seater trainers between March and August 1945.

Called the 'Reirensen' by the Japanese (or more often the Zero-Ren), the A6M2-K was pressed into service in a variety of roles, the most obvious of which was use as a kamikaze aircraft in the event of the Allied invasion of Japan.

The A6M2-N

Of much greater interest than the A6M2-K was the extremely remarkable A6M2-N. This was one of only two seaplane-fighters to see combat in World War II. (Inevitably the only other one was Japanese as well.)

In the autumn of 1940 the Imperial Navy, under the terms of the 15-Shi program, placed an order for a single-seater seaplane that could double as a fighter. Though the idea may sound bizarre, the reasoning behind the Navy's demand was not altogether unsound. The Japanese appreciated that in small-scale operations or during the initial phase of amphibious operations there could be a small period of time when neither carrier nor land-based fighters could cover units. In this case a seaplane fighter could be of great use as an interim measure until the arrival of first-line fighter aircraft. The Navy also appreciated that many Pacific islands enclosed calm water but were themselves too small to take runways. To fill the gap of patrolling from such islands and to cover small-scale operations the Japanese Navy wanted a seaplane that could be used as an offensive fighter.

There are obvious flaws in such a line of reasoning. If amphibious operations were needed then they automatically demanded as of right proper fighter cover, and if the islands and atolls were too small to take an airfield then the probability was that they were of little or no strategic value in any case.

Kawanishi was given the contract to build the seaplane fighter, but by the beginning of 1941 it became obvious that Kawanishi's purpose-built aircraft would take too long to get into production. The Navy therefore searched around for an improvised version and finally ordered Nakajima to produce a seaplane version of the

Below: **A6M2-Ks used for training.**

Below: **Another Zero trainer model.**

Above: **The A6M2-N, a seaplane fighter which never lived up to the promise of its design.**

Zero. Using the Model 11 as the prototype, in February 1941 Nakajima started work, though subsequent production was confined to Model 21s. All landing gear was removed and all wells on the undersurface of the wings were flushed over. The centrally-mounted drop tank was also discarded. After a series of tests Nakajima adopted the floats the company had used for its own E8N1 seaplane of 1934. This involved giving the Zero a very large central float to which it was attached by a single forward-sloping pylon fitted well forward on the Zero. Behind the pylon was a single, rather slender upward Vee strut. Outboard on the wings were two cantilevered floats. To compensate for the loss of the drop tank the central float itself was made into an auxiliary tank, the feed system being directed through the heavy pylon.

One would expect that the performance of the A6M2-N would have been considerably inferior to that of the A6M2, but surprisingly the seaplane fighter proved remarkably durable and nimble. The first A6M2-N, called by the Japanese the 2-Suisen, flew for the first time a matter of hours after Pearl Harbor and production versions exhibited the following characteristics:

Span	12.00m
Length	10.10m
Height	4.30m
Wing Area	22.44sq m
Wing Loading	109.70kg/sq m
Weight: Empty	1,912kg
Loaded	2,490kg
Maximum	2,880kg
Armament	As the standard A6M2.
Powerplant	940hp Sakae 12
Speeds: Maximum	271mph/436kph at 5,000m/16,405ft
Cruising	184mph/296kph
Rate of climb	6 minutes 43 seconds to 5,000m
Ceiling	10,000m/32,810ft
Range: Normal	714mph/1,150km
Maximum	1,107mph/1,882km

With these characteristics her performance was very formidable, and in the early days of the war she proved a match for American carrier-borne fighters. She also showed an ability to tackle the B-17 at 20,000ft, and one of the A6M2-N 'aces' had two confirmed B-17E kills. This was a very fine achievement, particularly when one remembers that the Flying Fortress commanded respect among orthodox Zeros. One A6M2-N even accounted for a Lightning, but this must be regarded as something of a freak.

The active service career of the A6M2-N was initially confined to two areas – the upper Solomons and the Aleutians. The 2-Suisens moved into the Solomons with the first wave of attacking Japanese forces, securing Florida Island and Tulagi on 3 May 1942. An air counterattack by the Americans next day accounted for four A6M2-Ns, but they were replaced immediately, and for the next three months the seaplane-fighter controlled the skies over the Solomons. They proved a match for the feeble performance the Allies put up in the area in mid-1942. But the A6M2-N could not meet the challenge posed by the Americans when the latter moved in force against Guadalcanal. The day before the landings on the island, American aircraft overwhelmed the seaplane fighters of the Yokohama Air Corps on Florida Island and the Japanese had to join battle with their conventional fighter aircraft.

The forces in the Aleutians proved to be longer lived. The Japanese took over various islands in the Aleutians as a long-stop for the approach to Japan from the north. These were the only pieces of American homeland territory to be taken over by enemy action in the course of the war. These islands were taken over in June 1942, but very quickly American pressure on the 5th Air Corps became intense. Between September 1942 and March 1943 – despite the appalling weather conditions – the American commitment of Fortresses, Catalinas and various other forms of aircraft gradually wore down the Japanese to the point where they voluntarily abandoned the islands. Despite successes, the A6M2-N could not stand up to orthodox air power, systematically exerted. The real truth of the situation for the A6M2-N was that despite the imagination of the Navy it never really had a role. Once the perimeter of Japanese conquests had been secured and 'hardened' the aircraft was superfluous. Even in the first stages of the war its value had been very marginal. After its defeats at either end of the Pacific the A6M2-N was reduced to second-line duties. Many were deployed on northern Borneo where they were committed to reconnaissance, convoy escort and antisubmarine duties. Most ended their operational careers as second-string interceptors either in the Kuriles, on Rabaul or in central Honshu where they were based on Lake Bawi near Kyoto. Several A6M2-Ns were used as trainers for the Kawanishi seaplane-fighter, the N1K1.

Nakajima built 327 A6M2-Ns. The last batch of 73 were hastened through to completion in September 1943 simply to clear production lines rather than for any importance the aircraft might possess. But the last production models were unique in that they were given full night-flying equipment and thus served as interceptors. The overall picture, however, was that the A6M2-N was an imaginative and highly proficient machine, but like the Japanese effort generally, improvisations could not match fighting power in depth.

The A6M5 Night Fighter

This was a modification peculiar to one unit, the 302nd Naval Air Corps. This Corps, based on Yokosuka, was established in March 1944 and served for the remainder of the war in defense of the Japanese homeland. In an effort to improve the Zero's performance as a night fighter the unit itself mounted a 20mm cannon behind the cockpit. It was angled at 30 degrees from the horizontal. It was the only version of a night-fighting Zero produced in the war.

2. Aircraft Production

There is no way of knowing the number of aircraft produced by Japan in the course of the Pacific War. The most authoritative source for Japanese production is *The United States Strategic Bombing Survey*, usually quoted by the best known commentator on the Japanese aviation services, Rene J Francillon, but even these two sources cannot reconcile certain discrepancies. The problem of accurately assessing Japanese production lies in the devastation caused by bombing to the Japanese aviation industry in the last year of the war. Figures from companies are at best unreliable. The Japanese source considered the most accurate is generally accepted to be the Government through its funding of production. According to this source the production of Zeros was as follows:

	Mitsubishi	Nakajima	Total
March 1939 – March 1942	722	115	837
April 1942 – March 1943	729	960	1,689
April 1943 – March 1944	1,164	2,268	3,432
April 1944 – March 1945	1,145	2,342	3,487
April 1945 – August 1945	119	885	1,004
	3,879	6,570	10,449

Other sources, while agreeing with the Mitsubishi figure, place production at Nakajima factories at 6215. If that figure was correct total production would be 10,094 aircraft.

The *Bombing Survey* gives the following figures as total Japanese aircraft production:

	1941	1942	1943	1944	1945	Total
Fighters	1,080	2,935	7,147	13,811	5,474	30,447
Bombers	1,461	2,433	4,189	5,100	1,934	15,117
Recce aircraft	639	967	2,070	2,147	855	6,678
Others	1,908	2,526	3,287	7,122	2,803	17,646
	5,088	8,861	16,693	28,180	11,066	69,888

It would seem, therefore, that Zeros totalled about 33 percent of Japanese fighter strength or nearly fifteen percent of all aircraft built in Japan between 1941 and 1945 (allowing for Zero production 1939–42 to be considered for 1941–42.)

It would appear to be impossible to accurately compute individual Mark and Model totals, but it is known that Mitsubishi and Nakajima between them built

2 A6M1 prototypes
17 A6M2 preproduction aircraft
2 A6M4 prototypes
93 A6M5c
1 A6M6c (by Mitsubishi) and
2 A6M8c prototypes.

No A6M8 aircraft were produced.
It is estimated that excluding prototypes 1634 A6M2s were built, and that of this total 740 were Model 21s. If these figures are anywhere near correct then it would be safe to assume that after the A6M5, the most numerous of the Zeros, came the A6M3.

The USSBS gives the total American aircraft production
for 1942 as 49,445
for 1943 as 92,196
for 1944 as 100,752.

To give American production figures is misleading in one respect. The American production effort was bent toward fulfilling the demands of two wars and to answer the needs of not only the American services, but also those of various Allied nations. Nevertheless, American production figures are of interest because, even allowing for the diversion of resources to the European war, the totals reflect the potential size of the American problem (in Japanese eyes) and the fact that the figures have as their base year a date later than those for Japanese aircraft, ie the USA was slower to build up its production to its full capacity than were the Japanese.

Below: **An A6M3 Model 32 identifiable because of its square wing tips.**

Total US production for selected aircraft was as follows:

B-17	Flying Fortress	12,731	Saw very little service in the Pacific.
B-24	Liberator	19,203	Standard heavy bomber in the Pacific.
B-25	Mitchell	9,816	Versatile medium bomber.
B-26	Marauder	5,157	As B-25.
B-29	Superfortress	3,970	Very heavy bomber. Dropped the A-bombs.
SBD	Dauntless	5,936	Standard dive bomber in 1941.
A-25	Helldiver	7,200	
TBF	Avenger	9,836	Standard torpedo bomber of the war.
F4U	Corsair	12,681	
F4F	Wildcat	7,005	Standard fighter in 1941.
F6F	Hellcat	12,272	Acclaimed best carrier fighter of the war.
P-38	Lightning	9,942	Alleged to have more Zero credits than F6F.
P-47	Thunderbolt	15,560	
P-51	Mustang	15,586	

Some of the totals are 'run-overs' from the war, but do not include production started after the end of hostilities.

3. The characteristics of the A6M3 Model 32 and the A6M5 Model 52

These were probably the two most numerous Marks of Zero produced in the war. The A6M5, of which there were four models, was certainly the most numerous of the Zeros, and the A6M3 probably outnumbered the A6M2. The A6M3 was not an improvement on the A6M2, but that more of the former were built can be explained by the higher tempo of construction at the time the A6M3 entered production than when the A6M2 was built.

	A6M3	A6M5
Span	11.00m	11.00m
Length	9.06m	9.12m
Height	3.51m	3.51m
Wing Area	21.53sq m	21.30sq m
Wing Load	107.40kg/sq m	128.30kg/sq m
Weights: Empty	1,807kg	1,876kg
Loaded	2,544kg	2,733kg
Maximum	2,644kg	2,952kg
Engine	One Nakajima NK1F Sakae 21 engine of 1,130hp	} common to both
Armament	Two 7.7mm machine guns Two 20mm cannon Two 30kg or 60kg bombs	} common to both
Maximum Speed	338mph	351mph
Cruising speed	230mph	common to both
Rate of climb	13.67m/sec	14.25m/sec
Service Ceiling	11,050m	11,740m
Range	1,477 miles	1,194 miles

Below: A captured Zero in US markings.

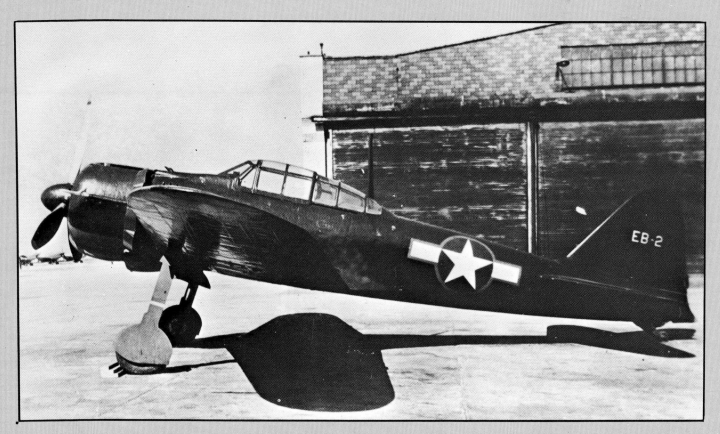

Acknowledgments

The author would like to thank the individuals and agencies listed below for the use of their photographs and artwork:

Bison Picture Library: pp 1, 7, 8–9.
Bob Snyder: pp 28, 45 (top right).
Fujifotos: pp 18–19 (top).
Grumman: p 33 (bottom).
John Batchelor: p 19 (center).

Kantosha Company: pp 9 (top), 12–13, 24–25, 25 (top left), 26, 28–29, 30, 31 (bottom left), 36–37 (all six), 41 (bottoms), 54–55 (bottom), 60.
Lockheed: pp 29, 32–33.
Mainichi: pp 56–57 (bottom).
Michael O'Leary: pp 22–23, 27 (center), 63.
National Air and Space Museum: pp 4–5, 41 (top).
National Archives: pp 21 (top), 37 (top left), 46, 48, 50, 51, 52 (center and bottom).
Royal Australian Air Force: pp 59 (top), 62.
Shizuo Fukui: pp 8, 14 (bottom).

Taylor Picture Library: pp 6–7, 11, 16, 20–21, 30–31 (top), 34–35, 40, 54–55 (top), 56–57 (top).
USAF: pp 25 (top right), 27 (top left both), 34 (top), 38–39, 49, 52 (top), 53, 59 (bottom).
US Navy: pp 15 (bottom), 18 (bottom two), 20 (top), 27 (bottom), 47, 64.
via Koku-fan: pp 2–3, 10, 14 (top), 15 (top both), 19 (bottom three), 41 (center), 42, 43, 54, 57 (center), 58, 61 (top).

Artwork

Mike Badrocke: cutaway on pp 42–43, line drawings on p 44.
Mike Bailey: Cover sideview.
Mike Trim: Sideview on p 45.

Above: **A Mitsubishi A6M5 Navy Type 0 Carrier Fighter Model 52 on a trial flight in the United States. The US markings have been partly painted out.**